Praise for Ada'
Emma's

MW00770929

"In his edited work, *Ada's Journal and Emma's Letters,* Andy Peck has given us a fascinating look into a Tennessee family's life in the mid-nineteenth century. With the addition of detailed research and a variety of family pictures, images, and interactive links highlighting the world they lived in, the Pecks come to life as we experience their perseverance among numerous tragedies. This will be a valuable addition to our Special Collections."

■ ALBERT L. LANG, Special Collections Librarian & Archivist, Mildred L. Iddins Special Collections, Stephens-Burnett Memorial Library, Carson-Newman University, Jefferson City, Tennessee

"*Ada's Journal* is a peek into the life of a child in the mid-1800s. A child born into a wealthy family who traveled from Tennessee where she was born to Louisiana to visit relatives and to the mountains of East Tennessee. The editor has provided photos and links to give the reader a glimpse into her world. In addition, he has transcribed letters her mother, Emma Peck wrote to her friend, Emma Allen, chronicling the loss of family and friends and the fear of the Civil War."

■ LINDA GASS, Archives Assistant, Carson-Newman University, Jefferson City, Tennessee

"Often when we look back in time we see faded pictures or a few sentences in a history book, and we miss the personal story. We fail to gain a perspective of the people or the time in which they lived. Andy Peck has provided both perspective and an excellent snapshot of the time in which Ada, Emma, and their family lived. Through his edited work *Ada's Journal and Emma's Letters,* we see the world of the Peck family; not as vague shadows in history but as real people with incredible highs and terrible lows. We gain a better understanding of the time and are able to walk vividly in their story. This work is a valuable part in telling the East Tennessee Story in the turbulent 1800s."

■ DAVID NEEDS
Carson-Newman University Instructor
Mossy Creek Historian
President of the Lakeway Civil War Preservation Association

Albert Lang (Left), Linda Gass (Middle), David Needs (Right)
Photos Courtesy of Carson-Newman University

Praise for Ada's Journal from a Homeschool Educator and Student

"*Ada's Journal and Emma's Letters* is a treasury of 19th century American history. The stories shared within these entries and correspondence take the reader into the very home of the Pecks, an affluent southern family. These excerpts of a time since past bring American history studies to life in a personal way as the reader comes to know Emma through her life marked by great joy and tragic sorrow. This book, beginning just before the Civil War and progressing throughout the 19th century, would be a vibrant addition to the library of any American history scholar."

■ SARAH L. ANGELL, Classical Home Educator, Scott Air Force Base, Illinois

"I thought Ada's Journals and Emma's Letters gave an engaging glimpse into a southern point of view during the Civil War. I have read lots of books from this time period, but most of them present things from only the Union perspective. It was interesting to think about things a bit differently, and also good to consider Ada's perspective on what was going on in the world at different ages."

■ JUSTICE BRATTON, 11 years old, homeschooled in Kathmandu, Nepal

Praise for Ada's Journal from a
Library Director and Military Retiree

"Mr. Peck has masterfully brought the past to life through the transcription of family documents. What's more, the inclusion of photos, maps and other primary source material flesh out the stories found within, and transport the reader back to the 1800s. This methodology and the inclusion of QR codes throughout *Ada's Journal* make for an interactive and engaging read. Any fan of genealogy, American history, or family lore is sure to find this book deeply captivating and satisfying."

> ■ RYAN JOHNSON, Library Director, BA Historical Studies, MA Library Science, O'Fallon, Illinois

"*Ada's Journal and Emma's Letters*, edited by Andy Peck, takes us on a journey from 1853 to 1855 presented by her mother, Emma Peck, via a journal written as a narrative by the young Ada. The journey provides insights to life during the first two years of Ada's life. We are taken on trips within Tennessee and between Tennessee and Louisiana. Today these journeys would be short, but in the 1850s transportation required much time between destinations. The diseases such as 'grip,' scarlet fever, dysentery, cholera and others often meant rapid death sentences during the period. The cholera epidemic and its history were informative. The biographical descriptions of Ada's relatives gave insight to the way death was treated. *Emma's Letters* gives knowledge of talk among the ladies of the era showing the antebellum, bellum and post bellum thoughts surrounding the Civil War. I thoroughly enjoyed the book and recommend it as a historical read."

> ■ KIM K. HILLARD, United States Air Force (Retired), Albuquerque, New Mexico

The Pecks of Mossy Creek

The Pecks of Mossy Creek series highlights the founding family of Mossy Creek (now Jefferson City), Tennessee and their ancestors and descendants. Adam Peck, Sr. and his wife Elizabeth (Sharkey) Peck pioneered west from their home in Fincastle, VA and floated down the Holston River on a flatboat. They settled Mossy Creek using a land grant of 5,000 acres Adam earned for his service in the Revolutionary War. As one of the Overmountain Men, he helped win the Battle of King's Mountain in 1780, and eight years later founded Mossy Creek. Adam and Elizabeth initially moved into an abandoned fort, and then built their own log cabin. He built a grist mill, which was the first mill in the area. At his wife's request, they built the first church in Mossy Creek and named it Elizabeth's Chapel in 1790. The Pecks had a number of slaves, and Elizabeth taught them to read and write along with their 12 children. One of these slaves was named

Uncle John, and they installed him as the first preacher. Rev. John Peck was called "the best human being there ever was," and the old log chapel became the foundation for the Methodist and Presbyterian churches in Jefferson City. In addition to the monument that says "Adam and Elizabeth Peck: Pioneers to the west from Virginia in 1788," the family burial plot in the Old Westview Cemetery in Jefferson City features a plaque that reads, "Pioneers of 19th Century Methodism at Mossy Creek."

The Pecks of Mossy Creek series seeks to highlight Peck family members and their stories through the years. Some notable Peck family members are:

- ❖ Jacob Peck, Sr. (1723-1801) – Adam Peck, Sr.'s father and Revolutionary War Veteran
- ❖ Lydia (Borden) Peck (1728-1800) – Adam Peck, Sr.'s mother and daughter of Benjamin Borden II and Zeruriah Winter
- ❖ Judge Jacob Franklin Peck (1779-1869) – Adam Peck, Sr.'s son, TN Supreme Court Judge, State Senator and Geologist
- ❖ Judge James Hawkins Peck (1790-1836) – Adam Peck Sr.'s son, War of 1812 Veteran, U.S. District Judge for Missouri

Cross Mountain Books is a proud supporter of the **Mossy Creek Foundation**. A portion of the proceeds from each book sold will be donated to the Mossy Creek Foundation in its efforts to revitalize the Historic Mossy Creek District in Jefferson City, TN. Learn more about this great project by visiting **mossycreekfoundation.org**.

MOSSY CREEK
FOUNDATION

Ada's Journal

and Emma's Letters

Ada Louise Peck

1853 — 1859

Ada's Journal
and Emma's Letters

The Civil War Era Journal and
Letters of Emma Peck

Edited by
Andy Peck

The Pecks of Mossy Creek
Andy Peck, Series Editor

Cross Mountain Books
Scott Air Force Base, Illinois
www.crossmountainbooks.com

Published by
Cross Mountain Books in Scott AFB, IL

Manufactured in the United States of America.

First Edition.

Cover & Frontispiece: Ada Louise Peck, oil on canvas. Painting by unknown, 1859. Photo of painting courtesy of Jack and Kathy Spratt.

Signed copies available. Books also available in quantity for promotional or premium use. For information, email info@crossmountainbooks.com.

www.crossmountainbooks.com
Facebook: fb.me/crossmountainbooks

Publisher's Cataloging-in-Publication Data
Names: Peck, Emma Elizabeth (Henderson), 1833-1900, author. | Peck, Andy
    (Thomas Andrew), 1981- , editor.
Title: Ada's journal and Emma's letters: the Civil War era journal and letters of
    Emma Peck / edited by Andy Peck.
Description: Scott AFB, IL : Cross Mountain Books, 2021. | Series: The Pecks of
    Mossy Creek. | Includes 70 illustrations: photos, maps, portraits. | Includes
    bibliographical references and index. | Summary: Ada's Journal is a travel and
    personal journal of Ada Louise Peck (1853-1859) written by her mother
    Emma Peck in pre-Civil War East Tennessee and Henderson Plantation in
    Louisiana. Emma's Letters includes 33 transcribed handwritten letters
    describing life before, during, and after the Civil War in Tennessee and
    Louisiana.
Identifiers: LCCN 2021904730 | ISBN 9781955121002 (pbk) | ISBN
    9781955121019 (hardcover) | ISBN 9781955121026 (ebook) | ISBN
    9781955121033 (audiobook)
Subjects: LCSH: Peck, Ada Louise, 1853-1859. | Peck, Emma Elizabeth
    (Henderson), 1833-1900. | Peck family. | Henderson family. | Louisiana—
    History. | North Carolina—History. | Tennessee, East—History. | BISAC:
    HISTORY / United States / 19th Century. | HISTORY / United States /
    State & Local / South (AL, AR, FL, GA, KY, LA, MS, NC, SC, TN, VA,
    WV). | HISTORY / Women.
Classification: LCC F442.1 P43 2021| DDC 975 P4--dc23
LC record available at https://lccn.loc.gov/2021904730

For you Sasha,
on the three-year anniversary of winning
the fight for your life against breast cancer, and
the fifteenth year of our marriage.
You are amazing!
I love you, and I
thank God for you.
Psalm 34:3

Figure 1 – 1920s Glen Ada Home, Wolf Creek, TN, Photo by Editor 29 Oct 2020

Video Journey

Travel virtually to numerous locations found in this book including Glen Ada, Mossy Creek / Jefferson City, the Wolf Creek Inn and more by watching *Ada's Journal and Emma's Letters: A Video Journey with Editor Andy Peck* by scanning the QR code below, or visiting: https://youtu.be/tKiot-ajk7s

Contents

Cross Mountain Books
Interactive Features

Throughout the book, you will notice QR Codes with the text. These are placed so that if you are interested to learn more about a topic or person, you can simply scan the Code. When you do, it will take you to a website that shares more information and photos about the topic.

With most smart phones, you can open the website associated with each QR code by simply opening your camera, and aiming it at the code. Let the camera focus on the code for a second, and it will bring up a prompt, asking if you would like to open the website. As the QR codes in this book link to third party websites, Cross Mountain Books is not responsible for the content or the stability of the links provided. If you do not have the ability to scan the codes, links are provided here for your convenience. Enjoy digging deeper into the following topics!

Page # - *Topic* - Website

1 — *Steamboats* - alabamapioneers.com/atlas-first-boat-ascend-tennessee-river-muscle-shoals/

8a — *Travel Map* - goo.gl/maps/aVfmMTtPhkvidNAT7

8b — *Loudon* - backroadplanet.com/drive-loudon-county-tennessee/

9 - *Solar Eclipse of 26 May 1854 — First to ever be photographed* - commons.wikimedia.org/wiki/Category:Solar_eclipse_of_1854_May_26_in_the_United_States

16a — *Hot Springs, NC* - ncpedia.org/hot-springs

16b — *Paint Rock, NC* - hotspringsnc.org/paint-rock/

21a — *Big Peck* - en.wikipedia.org/wiki/William_R._Peck

21b — *Lord Byron* - en.wikipedia.org/wiki/Lord_Byron

Acknowledgments

While conducting a telephone interview with my Great Aunt Arnette "Nette" Peck King in April 2017, I thought to ask her if she knew the name of her grandfather. She replied "Yes, it's Dr. Edward Jerome Peck…you know there is a monument to him in Wolf Creek, TN." I was flabbergasted, I had never heard his name, and I had never heard of Wolf Creek. [The monument is actually in Hot Springs, NC].

After I spoke with Aunt Nette, I contacted Betty Walker, president of the Wolf Creek Historical Society. Betty Walker lives in Wolf Creek, TN and owns the chaise couch used by Dr. Ed Peck to doctor his patients at the Mountain Park Hotel in Hot Springs, NC. She is a wealth of information about Wolf Creek history and I have since visited her home multiple times. She and her son Albert have been very gracious to me and have shed light on so many questions.

Betty told me to call Dorland Presbyterian, and I got in touch with Mary Gahagan. Mary told me to call Jacque Painter, a local historian and author of numerous books that mention the Peck Family.

I spoke with Jacque in May 2017, and she told me that Dr. Ed Peck delivered her grandma in Slabtown, TN and also her aunt at her home in Hot Springs, NC. I ordered several books from Jacque that have shed incredible light on my family and the area of Western North Carolina and Eastern Tennessee. Jacque shared with me that Jack and Kathy Spratt now own Glen Ada, the home and land once owned by Dr. Ed Peck, and before him, his father Dr. Isham Talbot Peck and his wife Emma Elizabeth (Henderson) Peck.

I called Jack and Kathy and they told me they were very interested in Peck history. Within days, Kathy mailed me photocopies of Ada's Journal, a number of letters between Emma Peck and Emma Allen, and even some old family photographs.

Betty introduced me to Ann (Kirkpatrick) Peck, wife of my second cousin, Arthur "Dwight" Peck. I travelled to Wolf Creek and met with Betty and Ann, had dinner with Jack and Kathy, and have had numerous telephone conversations with Jacque Painter over the last few years. With Betty as our navigator, Ann, Betty, and I drove all over Wolf Creek and Hot Springs. We found Dr. Ed Peck's grave in the Fairview Methodist Church graveyard and visited Paint Rock together.

By God's grace I was able to get in touch with a sweet and incredibly helpful woman named Linda Gass, long-time historian for Carson-Newman College in Jefferson City, TN. She spent hours of research and gave my family and me a personalized tour of Jefferson City, TN, even introducing us to Carson-Newman History Professor David Needs, who informed me about the civil war connections to Dr. Isham Talbot Peck, Ada's father.

I would like to take a moment and say THANK YOU to my Great Aunt Nette, and also: Betty Walker, Albert Walker, Mary Gahagan, Jacqueline Painter, Jack and Kathy Spratt, Ann (Kirkpatrick) Peck, Dorene "Dede" Dowling Rehkopf (3rd cousin), Helen Elizabeth "Bunny" Whitcomb Coates (3rd cousin), Linda Gass, David Needs, Albert Lang, and my editors Caroline Dobbs and Kaity S. Wiggins.

I would like to especially thank my family. My wife Sasha has been gracious as I have spent many late nights working on this book and also *Sawbones: The Life and Times of Dr. Isham Talbot Peck*. My sons Justice, Hudson, and Noble have been patient with me as I have played a few less games of basketball and baseball while working on these book projects. Thank you, my boys! I pray these books will bless you, your children, and many generations to come. This is our history! And a HUGE thank you to my sister Pattie Peck Harrelson, who painted the Henderson Plantation "Billy Buck" painting by special request!

Finally, thank you to my mom MaryAnn and dad Drew—thank you for always believing in me and loving me so well. I love you.

Thomas Andrew "Andy" Peck

John 3:30 ⨎

Editorial Policy

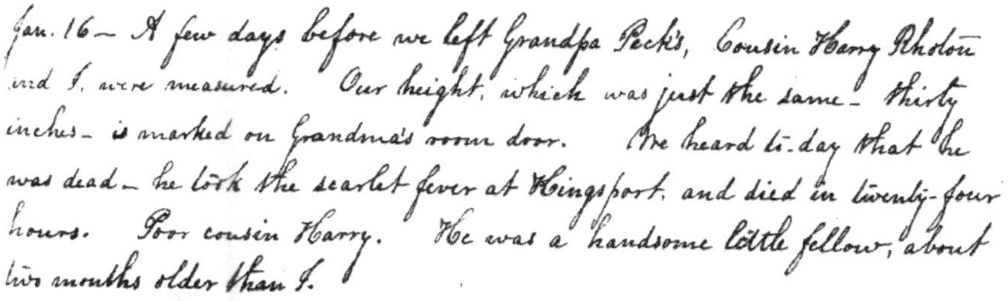
Jan. 16 – A few days before we left Grandpa Peck's, Cousin Harry Rhoton
and I, were measured. Our height, which was just the same – thirty
inches – is marked on Grandma's room door. We heard to-day that he
was dead – he took the scarlet fever at Kingsport, and died in twenty-four
hours. Poor cousin Harry. He was a handsome little fellow, about
two months older than I.

Figure 2 - 16 Jan 1855 Entry from Page 19 of Ada's Journal

Ada's Journal is 28 handwritten pages, written by Ada's mother, Emma Elizabeth (Henderson) Peck. *Emma's Letters* is made up of at least 84 individual original pages (33 letters and a telegram) stored in the Special Collections at University of Tennessee Libraries, Knoxville, in the Wolf Creek Papers, MS-3858. All words contained in this volume were transcribed by the editor. Emma's penmanship is quite legible, and so there are very few times when editorial guesses were necessary. Original copies obtained from friends and family were incomplete, with words in margins missing on some pages. A new and complete scan was made, with the assistance of Kyle Hovious (University of Tennessee – Knoxville Library Special Collections) in Jan 2021. This scan revealed all words that were close to the margins, and cleared up many questions.

Original punctuation is presented here. Emma used the underscore "_" quite often, sometimes as a comma, sometimes as a semi-colon, sometimes as a hyphen. She hyphenated words that we do not hyphenate today, i.e. "to-day" instead of "today." Her original punctuation has been maintained so the reader can see how the underscore was used by Emma.

Misspellings have been copied exactly as written, but I have inserted "[*sic*]" after the words in most instances. *Italicized* words in the course of the journal indicate an editorial insertion by me to help you understand or to point you to a QR code that will give additional insight about something mentioned in the journal. "[BEGIN PAGE #]" appears so that the reader can know on which page the text appears in the original manuscript.

Emma occasionally left large spaces between sentences in her writing. This may have indicated a new paragraph to the reader, but she could have been attempting to save paper by not dropping to the next line. These spaces have been retained and appear   as such.

At some point, someone wrote on the copies contained at the University of Tennessee Library, circled and underlined certain words, and made notes about locations that are mentioned—these notations are not included in this text, but they were informative at times.

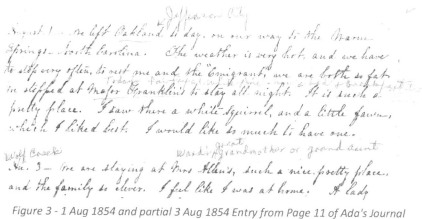

Figure 3 - 1 Aug 1854 and partial 3 Aug 1854 Entry from Page 11 of Ada's Journal

I, as the Editor, and Cross Mountain Books, as Publisher, have sought to present here an accurate transcription of the original source documents. All references to slavery, and words used to refer to black people, are presented in their original form for historical purposes. No offense is intended. We believe that all men are created equal, and at the outset of this book, we publicly condemn any form of racism. We believe that accurately viewing the past can help inform us today, and inspire us towards a better future.

Introduction

Ada's Journal gives us a window into history. She was a well-loved little girl who traveled with her family back and forth between E. Tennessee and the northeastern tip of Louisiana, starting in 1853. She experienced trials, health problems, and travel by rail, steamboat, and stagecoach.

This journal was transcribed by the Editor from a copy of the handwritten journal obtained from Mrs. Kathy Spratt of Wolf Creek, TN in May 2017. A copy is also contained in the Peck Family Papers, 1853-1902 in the Wolf Creek Papers, Betsey B. Creekmore Special Collections and University Archives at the University of Tennessee, Knoxville – Libraries. Ada was my 3rd Great Aunt and her father, Dr. Isham Talbot Peck, was my 3rd Great Grandfather. Ada lived from July 25, 1853 until March 27, 1859 (date from Emma in her April 22, 1859 letter). She was originally buried in a glass-top coffin in the front yard of Dr. Isham and Emma Peck at their home in Oakland, TN (close to Mossy Creek, modern day New Market / Jefferson City, TN).

This Oakland home was used as headquarters for the Union Army during the Civil War Battle of Mossy Creek. Soldiers helped themselves to Dr. Peck's guns, fishing poles, and more. There is correspondence recorded between the Union Army leadership going back and forth from the family's home in Oakland, TN and other military outposts.

In a book called *Bent Twigs in Jefferson County*, Jean Patterson Bible mentions Dr. Isham Peck's home and the "vault" where Ada lay on page 58. It says, "At about twelve noon the Yankee battery moved down the road and went into position in the front yard of doctor's home (Dr. Isham Peck – Mr. Neil Manley now lives where this house once stood) [*as of the year 2021 it is a medical center*]. During a lull in the firing of cannoneers[,] had a chance to look the house over. One Yankee said, 'this old English doctor is very nicely situated here. He has everything a sportsman could ask for, guns, fishing gear, etc., which we "borrow" from him. He must be of a rather eccentric nature as he has his family vault not twenty feet from the front door.' Actually, this was the grave of Dr. Peck's daughter, Ada, who died at the age of five on a trip south. Her body was returned and buried in a vault in the year in 1859. Later her remains were removed to Westview Cemetery where her tombstone can still be seen."

One other book, *Over the Misty Blue Hills* by Ruth Webb O'Dell, mentions little Ada on page 129. "Ada Peck, six years of age, was practicing her music at their winter home in New Orleans, when she suddenly ran to her mother and said, 'Mother, I'll never get to see the mountains again and I'll never see 'Mammy Allen' again.' (Referring to the wife of Reuben Allen [*Mary "Polly" (Jones) Allen*]). Six weeks later, the child died suddenly with brain fever."

Emma Peck wrote a letter to Emma Allen dated April 22, 1859. The letter details the events leading up to her quick death from cholera while they were living on Henderson Plantation in East Carroll Parish, Louisiana. The letter can be found in Appendix 3 of this volume.

Ada's mom, Emma Elizabeth (Henderson) Peck (born 1833 in Mississippi and died Aug. 9, 1900), was from East Carroll Parish, Louisiana and her parents were William Henderson (born 1798) and mom Louise (Donohue) Henderson (born 1813). She married Dr. Isham Talbot Peck on Oct. 12, 1848, when she was only 15 years old. Isham was born Feb. 23, 1811, and was 37 years old at the time. They married in East Carroll Parish, Louisiana, not far from Madison Parish, where his brother, William Raine Peck, lived at the time.

Ada's Journal was written by her mom, Emma, but from the perspective of little Ada. Ada was the first born of her siblings. Her parents would eventually have 9 children, and only 4 would survive into adulthood and be married. To read more about their family, see the forthcoming books *Sawbones*, and *He Loved the Folks* about Ada's father Isham and younger brother Ed. See back of book for more info.

Here are some family members mentioned in the journal:

Dr. Isham Talbot Peck's Family

Pa = Dr. Isham Talbot Peck (1811-1887) – Ada's father. A physician who served in the Army pre-Civil War, educated at Greenville College (now Tusculum University), & wrote under the pen name "Sawbones" (an old term for a doctor) to local paper *The Morristown Gazette*

Grandpa Peck = Judge Jacob Francis Clayton Peck (1779-1869) – Tennessee Supreme Court Justice and Senator, & an amateur geologist

Grandma Peck = Sophia Westener (Talbott) Peck (1788 – 1871)

Aunt Jane = Eliza "Jane" Talbot Peck (1812-1868) – Isham's sister, and wife of Madison H. McEffee (1809-1833)

Cousin Ellen = Juliet "Ellen" McEffee (1833-?) – Jane's daughter

Aunt Juliet = Juliet N. (Peck) Rhoton (1816-1864) — Isham's sister

Henry Clay = Juliet's son (14 May 1853 – 29 Dec 1854)

Uncle Doctor = Juliet's husband, Dr. John F. Rhoton

Uncle Bill = Gen. William Raine Peck, "Big Peck" (1818-1871) – Known as the largest Civil War General (6' 6" and 330 lbs.) and final commander of the famed "Louisiana Tigers." He owned a sprawling mansion called "The Mountain" in Madison Parish not far from the Milliken's Bend on the Mississippi River

Uncle "Jack" = Isham's brother John Henry Peck (1826-1894)

Aunt "Pattie" = Isham's sister Martha Ann Featherstone Peck (1819-1882) – Lived with her brother "Jack" and their parents.

Emma Elizabeth (Henderson) Peck's Family

Grandpa Henderson = William Henderson (1798 – Sep 1867) – Owned 2,702 acres in the "Henderson Community" in East Carroll Parish, LA.[1] Referred to as "Grandpa Hendy" at one point in the book.

Grandma Henderson = Louise (Donohue) Henderson (4 Mar 1813 – 13 Feb 1897). See her obituary in Appendix 7.

---

[1] *A Place to Remember: East Carroll Parish, LA 1832-1976,* by Georgia Payne Durham Pinkston, 1977, Pg 23.

Figure 4 - Dr. Isham Peck circa 1861,
Photograph by New Orleans
Photographer Samuel Anderson

Figure 5 - Dr. Isham Peck circa 1875,
Photo from More Reflections of Our
Heritage, A Bicentennial Edition, Cocke
County, 1995. p74

Figure 7 - Emma Peck circa 1875, From
More Reflections of Our Heritage, A
Bicentennial Edition, Cocke County, 1995.
p74

Figure 6 - Emma Peck circa 1865, Photo
from Arnette Peck Collection, Used by
Permission

About the Author

Emma Elizabeth (Henderson) Peck, was born 1833 in Mississippi and died August 9, 1900, in Florida. She lived 67 years before dying in Lake City, FL where she lived with one or more of her sons. She was from East Carroll Parish, Louisiana and her parents were William Henderson and Louise (Donohue) Peck.

Her dad was born in Mississippi and was listed as a "Planter" on the 1860 census of Ward 1 in the Carroll Parish of Louisiana. Nothing is known currently about William's parents, but we do know that he had a twin brother (information found in *Ada's Journal*). Her mom, Louise Henderson ("Louisa" on the census) is listed as a "Housewife" and born in Missouri. The Tourette Map of 1853 (see fig. 10) shows the sprawling Henderson Plantation, bordering the Mississippi River's western banks. "According to local courthouse records . . . Samuel Galloway, for whom Galloway Bayou is named, sold land in 1833 to William Henderson."[2] William owned at least 2,702 acres in 1843.[3] In *A Place to Remember*, we learn that William and his brother-in-law, Horace Prentice, were in business together (pg 22). In 1860, Joseph Menn, published a book called *The Large Slaveholders of Louisiana-1860*. It says that as of 1860, William Henderson owned 143 slaves with 36 slave dwellings on his plantation. Land and personal property worth $349,010.[4] When the Civil War was over, and the government was trying to sort out those who were Confederate sympathizers vs. who had supported the Union, this book would have been a smoking gun against the Hendersons due to their large slaveholding.

---

[2] *A Place to Remember: East Carroll Parish, LA 1832-1976*, by Georgia Payne Durham Pinkston, 1977, Pg 21.

[3] Ibid, Pg 23.

[4] Adjusted for inflation, this is the equivalent of $11 million in 2021

Emma was close to her mom and dad, and frequently lived with them on the Henderson Plantation, even after being married. She also traveled there with her family multiple times (even though they had one or two homes in East Tennessee). After the Civil War, the Henderson family, and eventually Emma herself, claimed that in February 1863 a detachment of General Ulysses S. Grant's Army, stationed at Milliken's Bend, took from Henderson Plantation:

30,000 bushels corn, at $1 each = $30,000

60 head of cattle, 350 pounds each, at 8 cents a pound = $1,680

120 cords of wood (rails) at $3 each = $360

As administratrix of her father's estate, Emma sued the United States Government for $32,040 according to the act of March 3, 1883, and the act of March 3, 1887. The case was finally tried on 20 November 1900 (three months after Emma died). The court determined that "it does not appear that the claimant's decedent, William Henderson, was loyal to the Government of the United States throughout the war for the suppression of the rebellion." They also determined that the value of the items taken was $8,960 rather than $32,040.[5] Because William, his wife Louise (aka Gam), and daughter Emma were all gone when it finally went to trial, it is unclear if any money was ever given to the family. It would seem that the money was not, because the court determined that the Hendersons were Confederate sympathizers. I share this story in part because of the historical value, but also to demonstrate that Emma was a fighter. Later in life, she is a party to a number of lawsuits in East Tennessee, fighting for land that belonged to her husband Isham, which she wanted to keep in the family.

---

[5] 57th Congress, 1st Session. Senate, Document No. 91. Filed 3 Dec 1900.

Emma married Dr. Isham Talbot Peck on October 12, 1848, when she was only 15 years old. Isham was born February 23, 1811, and was 37 years old. They married in East Carroll Parish, Louisiana. By 1850, they lived in the Western District of Carroll Parish and are listed just after Emma's parents on the census. Isham was listed as a Physician on the census, which was taken on 22 September 1850. No value was listed for the real estate of Isham, but William shows a value of $160,000 in land. They must have been living on the Henderson Plantation with her family.

Figure 8 - 1850 census - Western District, Carroll Parish, LA

In 1853, the year Ada was born, *The Congressional Globe, Vol 2, Part 1*, Pg 349 notes under the Petitions section, "The following petitions and memorials were presented under the rule, and referred to the appropriate committees: [. . .] By Mr. Moore, of Louisiana; The petition of Hannibal Faulk and others, and Mrs. Emma Peck, in relation to their claims in the Bastrop Grant, in Louisiana." Felipe Enrique Neri, The Baron de Bastrop, was granted two million acres by the King of Spain in the 1790s, and his goal was to bring in 500 settlers to colonize the area. [6] The Hendersons, and then the Pecks, must have lived on land that was originally a part of the Bastrop Grant.

Between 1903 and 1915, the US Department of the Interior and the US Geological Survey office marked key points throughout

---

[6] https://www.thenewsstar.com/story/news/local/2015/12/03/west-carroll-parish-history/76738424/, accessed 27 Feb 2021.

Louisiana. In their 1916 Bulletin 634 they list the following information for Geological Survey Bench Marks placed at Henderson Plantation. Henderson Plantation was located next to "Eagle Bend Quadrangle."

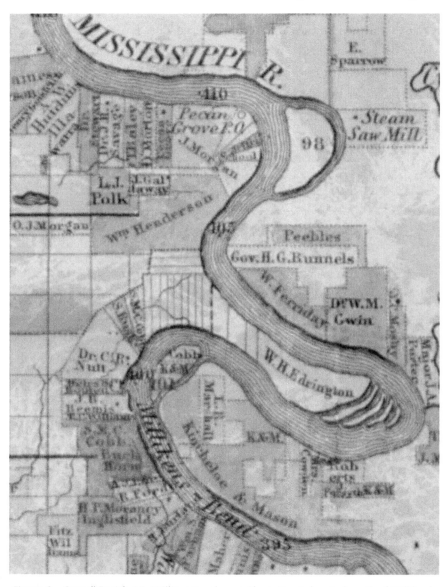

Figure 9 – Carroll Parish, LA, William Henderson Plantation is located north of Milliken's Bend, site of famous Civil War Battle. La Tourrette, John. La Tourrette's reference map of the state of Louisiana: from the original surveys of the United States, which show the townships, sections, or mile squares, Spanish grants, settlement rights & c., also the plantations with the owners names engraved thereon. *New Orleans: John La Tourrette, 1853. Map. https://www.loc.gov/item/2006629768/.*

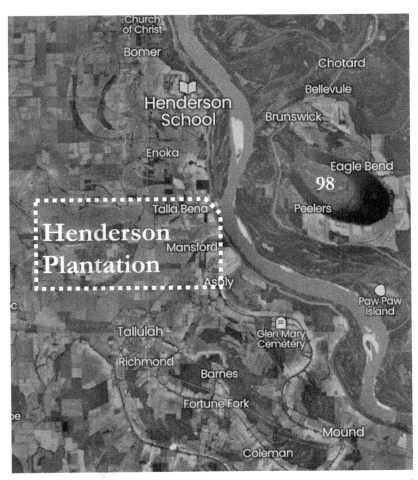

Figure 10 – Modern Satellite Map of Madison Parish, LA. Approximate location of Henderson Plantation notated by dashed lines and "98" added indicating likely location of historical Island 98. Notice "Henderson School" north of location. "Henderson Island" (not shown) is just to the northeast, and Vicksburg just to the southeast. Talla Bena and Mansford Plantations were likely comprised of what was once Henderson Plantation.

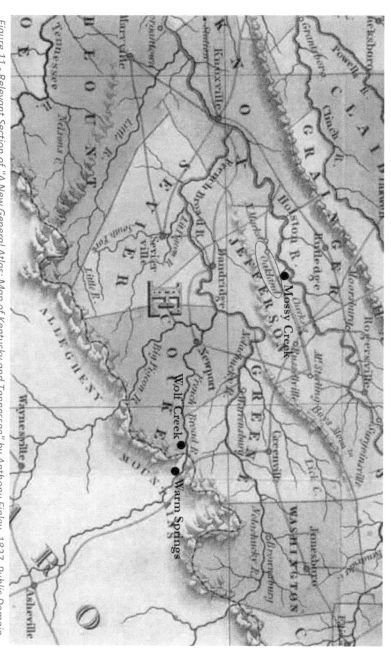

Figure 11 - Relevant Section of "A New General Atlas: Map of Kentucky and Tennessee" by Anthony Finley, 1827. Public Domain. Additions to map by editor: Circle around Oakland, Cities of Mossy Creek (Modern day Jefferson City), Wolf Creek, and Warm Springs (Modern day Hot Springs, NC). Notice that Oakland is a geographical location, not just a name for the Peck home.

Figure 12 - Modern day map of Eastern Tennessee including Jefferson City and Wolf Creek, Google Earth, 4 Mar 2021

After marrying in 1848, Emma and Isham lived alternately on Henderson Plantation in Louisiana and their farm they established near New Market, close to Jefferson City, TN (called "Oakland" in *Ada's Journal* and listed on the 1827 TN map in Figure 11). On 21 Aug 1854 they picked out "Glen Ada," a piece of land in Wolf Creek, TN, and decided to build their "Mountain Home" there. They bought thousands of acres all around Glen Ada from their new friends The Allens. Emma became close friends with all of the Allens, but especially Emaline "Emma" Allen. Emma Allen was born 2 May 1821 and died Sep 1888. The majority of the letters in this book were written by Emma Peck to Emma Allen. Original letters were found, photographed, and later transcribed by the editor at the University of Tennessee Library in Knoxville, TN. The letters are found in MS 2852, Box 1. After Emma Allen's death, Emma Peck and mother Louise began sending letters to Maggie (Gentry) Allen. Maggie was married to Emma Allen's nephew David W. (D.W.) Allen. Maggie was born 24 Jan 1858 in Arkansas and died 27 Dec 1934 in Wolf Creek, TN.

In relation to the founding family of Mossy Creek, Isham was the son of Judge Jacob Peck, who was the son of Adam Peck, Sr. (founder). Emma was Isham's third wife. During her lifetime, she gave birth to nine children. Here are their names and dates. Full biographies can be found in these books by the same editor and Cross Mountain Books: *Sawbones: The Life and Times of Dr. Isham Talbot Peck* and *He Loved the Folks: Dr. Edward Jerome Peck of Hot Springs, NC.*

1) Ada Louise Peck (25 Jul 1853 – 27 Mar 1859)
2) William "Willy" Henderson Peck (30 Nov 1855 – 1 May 1871)
3) Charles "Charley" Talbot Peck (16 Nov 1857 – 18 Feb 1882)
4) Dr. Edward Jerome Peck (14 Oct 1859 – 7 Jun 1927)
5) Ashby H. Peck (1862 – 27 Nov 1887)
6) Louis Sharkey Peck (15 May 1865 – 27 Jun 1937)

7) Paul Eve Peck (23 Mar 1869 – 22 Nov 1922)

8) Helen Emma Peck (24 Nov 1871 – 27 May 1887)

9) Robert Lee Peck (29 Apr 1874 – 10 Jan 1938)

Ada was born at Oakland in Jefferson City, TN and was the pride of her parents. She traveled all over with them, back and forth from Tennessee to Louisiana, but also to Virginia to visit her Grandpa Peck. She died from cholera at the age of five. This journal chronicles the first two years of her life.

Willy was born in Louisiana, most likely on the Henderson Plantation. His mom bragged about him and his intellect in the letters contained in this book. He tragically committed suicide by taking laudanum at the age of 15.

Charley was born in Louisiana and became a lawyer at a young age, but died in the streets of Cincinnati, OH of "an apoplectic fit" at the age of 22. His brother Dr. Ed Peck traveled to Cincinnati and arrived before Charley died, but he was unable to save him.

Dr. Edward "Ed" Jerome Peck married and divorced by 1900. He served the people of Hot Springs, NC and the surrounding area for approximately 40 years. He was the resident physician at the famous Mountain Park Hotel and he also worked for the railroad as a railroad surgeon. He died at the age of 67 and had four children (including the editor's Great Grandfather Percy Ward "Pop" Peck). A monument was erected and stands today in his honor at the Fairview Methodist Church in Hot Springs, NC.

Ashby ran a small newspaper in Wolf Creek called "The Mountain Boomer," and later became a telegraph operator. After moving to Jacksonville, FL for his job as a telegraph operator with the Florida Railway and Navigation Company, he committed suicide by taking a lethal dose of laudanum. He had attempted suicide six weeks prior by the same method, but was resuscitated by physicians and friends.

When news reached Wolf Creek of his son's suicide, his dad Isham fell dead. Ashby was 25 years old when he died.

Louis was born right at the end of the Civil War. He moved to Tallahassee, FL in 1886 at the age of 21, married Frances "Fannie" Perkins two years later, and served as a trainmaster for the Seaboard Air Line Railway. There is no evidence that Louis and Fannie had children. He died at the age of 72 from unknown causes.

Paul became the postmaster for Wolf Creek at the age of 16, then a depot agent at the Newport, TN railroad office at the age of 19. He married Ella R. King in Columbia, FL on 7 Jan 1891 and they had their only son, Richard King Peck on 4 Nov 1891 in Lake City, FL. He also became a ship chandler, supplying goods to the ships in and around Jacksonville, FL. He died in 1922 at the age of 53 after a nervous breakdown (according to his obituary).

Helen was born at Glen Ada. She was born just seven months after Willy took his own life. At the age of 15 years old, her parents enrolled her in the Salem Girls Academy in Winston-Salem, NC, a Moravian school. During her first semester, she died after a two-week illness with her parents by her side. Her body was returned to Tennessee for burial. Upon his return home to Wolf Creek, Isham climbed to the top of the mountain across from Glen Ada and erected a large white cross at the spot where Helen would retreat for reading and study. It was such a prominent cross that the mountain became known as "Cross Mountain" and the cross became a boundary marker for the border between Tennessee and North Carolina.

Robert, the youngest, was most certainly named after the Civil War Confederate General Robert E. Lee. He was born when Isham was 63 and Emma 41 years old. He followed three of his older brothers and worked for the railroad. He married Isabella Elizabeth "May" Purden on 9 Jan 1901. He became a train inspector and by 1910 they were living in Sanford, FL, with their two children Helen and Lee. In

1920 he was a train dispatcher. In 1938, he got appendicitis and then died following an operation in Sanford, FL. His obituary says he served as the Chief Dispatcher for the Atlanta Coast Line Railroad for 20 years and had worked for the railroad for 40 years.

Emma and husband Isham lived in Wolf Creek for much of their later years, making their permanent home there. But after Isham's death in 1887, Emma eventually moved to Lake City, FL, and lived with son Paul, his wife Ella, and their little boy Richard. For some of her later years, her mom "Gam" and Ella's mom "Mrs. King" all joined Paul and family in Lake City. She also had a talking parrot (possibly the one Ada received as a present in 1855). Her mom died on 13 Feb 1897 at the age of 84 (born 1813). Emma died just three years later on 9 Aug 1900 when she was 67 years old.

Figure 13 - "People travel by stagecoach for dinner at the Imperial Hotel in Cookeville, [TN]." https://www.tnmagazine.org/ridesharing-1800s-style/, accessed 26 Dec 2020

Figure 14 - The Stagecoach. , 1880. [Cincinnati, Ohio: Krebs Lith. Co., about] Photograph.
https://www.loc.gov/item/2018756637/, accessed 1 Apr 2021

Ada Louise Peck. My Journal. [*1853*]

At Oakland, Tennessee, on the 25th of July, 1853, about 2 o'clock in the morning, I was born. When I was a few hours old, Father put a little switch by my pillow, that had been seasoning for me. For sometime all the days are pretty much alike – I was troubled a good deal with the colic, and was dosed a good deal. When I was only seven weeks old, I commenced my travels. On the ninth of September, in a hard storm, we took the stage for Knoxville. It was the first time I had ever seen Mother have on a bonnet, and I stared at her so long, she thought I did not know her. I layed part of the time on my breast on a pillow, and as I would raise up my head to look about me, Uncle Bill would laugh, and say I looked like a Lizzard [*sic*]. We took a steamboat

SCAN ME

[*Scan QR code to learn about the first steamboats over Muscle Shoals*] at Knoxville for Decatur [TN]_ Railroad from there to Tuscumbia [AL] _ and four days of staging from there to Lagrange [TN] _ and railroad for the last time, to Memphis.

SEP 1853 ADVENTURE

Start: Jefferson City, TN
Stagecoach to Knoxville, TN
Steamboat to Decatur, TN
Railroad to Tuscumbia, AL
Stagecoach to La Grange, TN
Railroad to Memphis, TN

Figure 15 - https://condrenrails.com/MRP/Other-Passenger-Stations/Memphis-Charleston.htm, accessed 4 Jan 2021

Figure 16 – "A Memphis and Charleston Railroad train crosses the Tennessee River at Florence, Lauderdale County, ca. 1890. The railroad was the first rail link between the Mississippi River and the Atlantic Ocean and was a key transportation route for the Confederacy during the Civil War." Courtesy of the Alabama Dept of Archives and History and the Encyclopedia of Alabama, accessed 26 Dec 2020.

Figure 17 - Typical stagecoach during 1800s, Google image

It was such an unpleasant trip, it liked to have killed us all. The staging made me so sore, that every night I had to be bathed in warm water: and then I never rested well for the beds were full of bugs._one night they were so bad, mother were so bad, mother

sat up and held me all night. Uncle Bill fared better than any of us, for he slept in the stage. The country was very poor [BEGIN PAGE 2] and desolate looking, that we travelled over. The people not only had mean houses, but they had no idea of keeping them clean, or of fixing anything fit to eat. One night we did not get to our stopping place, till in the night, and having a bad attack of the colic, and no house being

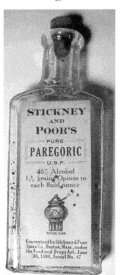

near, Pa guessed at the quantity of Paregoric, and got water out of a mud hole, to give me. It was then dark, and we had five miles to go, over a bad road _ Pa and Uncle Bill walking ahead in their

Figure 18 - 19th Century Paregoric bottle. Contained opium. Dosage amounts on back of bottle (below). www.peachridgeglass.com, accessed 26 Dec 2020

shirt sleeves, that the driver might see where to drive.

I got so dirty on the railroad, the cinders were all over my head and face, but as I had little or no hair, I was easily made clean after reaching Memphis. When the steam whistle would blow, I would look right at Mother, and if she was not frightened_very well_I did not mind either. Papa bought me so many pretty things in Memphis._ A set of Coral beads_ a little diamond ring_ and a newfashioned self-rocking cradle, which makes me sleep so sound. I had two likenesses taken of me, and sent one back to Aunt Pattie, by Uncle Jack_ who never called me anything but little Punkins_ and sent one by Uncle Bill_ who left us at Memphis_ to Grandma, who had not seen me since I was a little tiny baby. We were obliged to stay in Memphis a week. The yellowfever was so bad all along the river, we were afraid to go home. I had to stay in a little room all the time, and not being used to coal fires, I took a very bad cold, that [BEGIN PAGE 3] liked to have killed me, landing at home off the boat James Robb, at midnight, made me much worse, and I had to be blistered on my breast, before I got well. I then brightened up, and commenced looking about to see how I liked home. I never tired of looking at the chickens and turkeys. I played with the

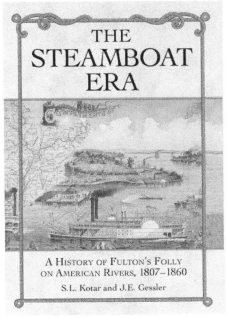

THE **STEAMBOAT ERA**

A HISTORY OF FULTON'S FOLLY
ON AMERICAN RIVERS, 1807–1860
S.L. Kotar and J.E. Gessler

Figure 19 - Book about steamboats from era

dogs and cats_ rode in my willow carriage_ but the most pleasant time was spent in the kitchen, watching the old cook.

When I was about six months old, Uncle Bill gave me three bales of fine cotton, which brought me more than a hundred dollars. With half of it I bought my Grandpa and Grandma Peck, two large rocking chairs_ The other half I spent in little presents to my Aunt Pattie. This winter Uncle gave me such a pretty pair of thin gold band bracelets, and a pair of gold armlets with pretty stones in them.

Figure 20 - General William Raine Peck, "Big Peck." Known by Ada as various names, but especially Uncle Bill. Photo circa 1870, Public Domain.

1854

[*Louisiana*] March 25_I am now a respectable sized girl (I always was fat, weighing, when I was born more than eight pounds) of eight months, and weigh about twenty-three pounds, and am twenty-eight inches high. I have quit that ugly habit of putting every thing in my mouth that was given to me, to play with. I take two naps every day, when I am well. After dinner (which does not deserve that name, for I get precious little to eat) Mother sometimes takes me riding on old black [BEGIN PAGE 4] pony, and with Chat leading, and Julia and Alice keeping up on each side of me, and all talking at once, I am highly delighted. Although I ride till I get tired, there is always a fuss, when I have to get off

Apr. 6_ I was made so happy today, by Grandpa [William Henderson] coming home, and bringing me a pretty little carriage, which is large enough to last me untill [*sic*] I get tired of it. Yesterday I took a long ride in the big buggy. I wish you could have seen my pittiful [*sic*] little face when I was taken out. Old pony had to be goodnight before I could be quieted. I am a little sick, I think I am teething, but there is no telling, for Mother has been daily watching for the first tooth, ever since I was two months old. When it is warm, I always take a walk before breakfast, nearly always with Grandma [Louise Henderson], to see the cows and calves, and sometimes drinking some milk. At the table, Grandma gives me bread to feed the cats, but I had much rather eat it myself, and generally make an attempt to do so. A few evenings ago Mother showed me the moon, and this evening, while riding in my little carriage, I found it again, without any one telling me.

Apr. 25_ I am nine months old today, and what is more interesting, my first tooth made its appearance today. I was carried round for every one to have a look at it. [BEGIN PAGE 5]

May 3_ We left Louisiana for Tennessee [*Scan QR code for travel stops*], on the fine boat, R. J. Mard, today. I was waked up early, for we saw the boat's smoke round the point, and by the time I was dressed, she was at the landing. She was running very fast, so we made a quick trip to Smithland. I tried to get acquainted with all the children on board, and could make as much noise squealing, as any of them. We stayed one night at Smithland, and next morning took a boat for Nashville. I like Nashville very well. There was a gallery up stairs, where I could stand and look down on horses_ dogs_ and people, for hours at a time. _ and I expect it was staying out there so much, that made me take cold. We stayed three days, then took the [*railroad*] cars for Loudon [*Scan QR code for a modern-day tour of Loudon*] and the Stage from there to Knoxville. The scarlet fever was bad at several places, so that we could not stop to rest. I got very tired in the ears, I was not used to sitting so long in one place. On our way up the Mississippi, the "Mard" stopped at Memphis a while, and my Grand Uncle (my Grandfathers twin brother) came on board to see us. As soon as I saw him, I  wanted to go to him, I thought it was my Grandpa. They look very much alike, and I think it something remarkable, that I, so young, should have seen the resemblance. I cried for him when he went away. [BEGIN PAGE 6]

May.12_This morning papa hired a carriage and four horses to take us from Knoxville to grandpa's, and this evening about sunset, we arrived at beautiful Oakland. I am now in the room in which I was born. Grandma and all, were so glad to see me.

May 25_ I am ten months old today. I like Oakland so much. It is such a pretty place to ride round in my little box carriage, that Papa and Uncle Jack made for me. The yard is a perfect strawberry patch. I go out several times a day, to get as many as I want. I like to be led about through the patch so I can hunt for them_ and sometimes I go in my carriage. The chairs for Grandpa and Ma came a few days ago. They are very comfortable. Mother wrote to my Louisiana Grandma today, and I sent my mark, too, which was my little fat hand (pin cushion, as Aunt Patt calls it) dipped in ink, and spread out on the paper_ Then Papa took one of my little tapering fingers, dipped it in ink, and made me write_ Ada. I have a cotton doll now, and I go to sleep with it in my arms. How I do love to be out of doors, if I had my way I never would come in the house.

SCAN ME

May 26_I was as busy as any body looking at the Eclipse of the sun, today. [*Scan QR code for actual photos of the 16 May 1854 Solar Eclipse, the first one to ever be photographed*] / [BEGIN PAGE 7]

June 7_ I rolled out of bed today, but was not hurt. I was very much frightened and screamed very loud.

June 13_ We started on our mountain trip today, after dinner. Mary was on Aunt Patt's riding pony, and I was very much amused, looking at her through the little glass windows. We are on our way to see Grandpa [*Judge Jacob*] Peck, who has not seen me since I was seven weeks old. He is in Carroll County, Virginia, where a Copper mine has been found, and Grandpa owns part of it.

June 23_We are at a place, known as Early's Spring. We expected to find Grandpa here, but he had left a few days before. He heard by accident, that we were on our way to this place, and turning back, came a few hours after us, today. I took quite a fancy to him, and commenced at once to get acquainted. We had a very pleasant trip from Oakland. here. The carriage is large and roomy, and I would sit on the floor and play with my toys and rocks, when I get tired of being held. Every day at dinner time, we stopped at a Spring, and in a good shade, if we could find it, and while all helped about our dinner, I would play to my heart's content in the dirt. How happy I was, and what a good appetite I had_ and then how funny it was, cleaning the dinner_ things and me. When there was no stream close by, I was stripped and put in the horse bucket. I was always [BEGIN PAGE 8] glad when we were ready to start, but thought resting time ought to come oftener. I fatten every day. I am learning to do a great many smart thing. I mimic the different animals, and snap my fingers at everything I see. I am so cross when we have to stay all night in the little towns, but am in a fine humour all the time, if we stop at pretty country places, where there are plenty of goats and ducks for me to look at. At Jonesborough [TN] I went visiting for the first time. I was so bad and cross, Mother said it would be the last time_ and Aunt Patt said it wouldn't. I have been very sick for several days. I suffer a great deal with my gums. We rested here one day, then, with Grandpa, started for Oakland.

June 25_ I am eleven months old today_ and am not near so fat as I was sometime ago. We are staying at Capt Raper's, a very pleasant place.

July 1_ We reached Kingsport [TN], here my Aunt Jane lives, to-day. It would have been very pleasant, travelling, if it had not been so hot. This week there has been some of the hottest weather known in this country, for years. When we stopped for dinner, I had fine plays with Grandpa, on the gras [*sic*] and rocks. I noticed every thing, well, would point to the springs and trees, and took great delight in playing in the water. I came into town with nothing on, but a little shirt. [BEGIN PAGE 9] All were very glad to see me, but laughed at the way I was dressed. I weigh 24 ½ pounds.

July 10_ We arrived at Oakland today_ all tired. We staid [*sic*] a week at Aunt Jane's. I was so well pleased I did not like to come away. Cousin Ellen came with us. I was glad to see Oakland again, I was getting very tired of travelling, although we had so much fun sometimes. If we came to a good blackberry patch, such picking and eating we would have, and I, as busy as any. We found three letters here, from my Louisiana Grandma and Grandpa. When Mother tells me, "they sent kisses to me," I always kiss the letters.

July 22_ We had a great fish_ fry to-day, at a pretty shady place on the Holston river, and plenty of fine fish. I had a great deal of fun playing in the dirt, then washing in the river. We received a letter this evening from Grandma. She says she is going to give a grand dinner on my birthday.

July 23_ We went to the spring a few evenings ago, and were caught in such a dreadful storm, but I did not mind it much, for I soon went to sleep, but when I waked, we were running to the house, and mother had me nearly smothered, trying to keep the rain off me.

Figure 21 - Peterson's Magazine. United States: C.J. Peterson, 1883.

Blackberry Cordial.—To one quart of blackberry-juice add one pound of white sugar, half an ounce of grated nutmeg, and half an ounce of pulverized cinnamon. Tie the spice in a fine muslin bag, boil the whole and skim it. When no more scum rises, set it away to get cold, and add one pint of best brandy. Cloves and allspice may be added in the proportion of a quarter of an ounce of each.

[BEGIN PAGE 10]

July 25_ I am one year old to-day. It has been a beautiful day, and we took dinner out in the yard, under a fine old Oak. I sat up to the table, by myself, for the first time in my life. My health was drunk in Blackberry Cordial, and I drank a good deal, myself, out of my little tumbler, which I can hold. A plate full of little biscuits was set by me, although I have one jaw tooth, I could not eat any of them. I was dressed in white at dinner, and had on all my jewelry. I knew a great

deal of attention was paid to me_ I was very proud of it, and tried to see how good I could be. In the evening it was so hot, I took off all my clothes, but a shirt. Papa put up a fine swing here. Grandpa and I have some fine swings_ he ties me in with his handkerchief. I like it so well, there is always a fuss, when I am taken out.

Figure 22 - 1800s Mother Goose's Nursery Rhymes

July 29_ Uncle Jack gave me his first present today_ It is an interesting little book called_ Mother Goose. I have been kissing the pictures all evening. I went to town this evening, and behaved myself, while we were waiting for the mail, which brought us another letter from Grandma. [BEGIN PAGE 11]

August 1_ We left Oakland today, on our way to the Warm Springs_ North Carolina. The weather is very hot, and we have to stop very often, to rest me and the "Emigrant," we are both so fat. We stopped at Major [*Isaac White Rogers (W.R.)*] Franklin's [*River View / The Fairfax Inn in White Pine, TN*] to stay all night. It is such a pretty place. I saw there a white squirrel, and a little fawn, which I liked best. I would like so much to have one.

Figure 23 – The Fairfax Inn located at 380 Cody Rd., White Pine, TN. It was a wedding gift from Isaac's father Lawson D. Franklin in 1853.
https://www.oldhousedreams.com/2011/03/07/1855-greek-revival-white-pine-tn/, accessed 3 Jan 2021

Clifton Johnson, Highways & Byways

Figure 24 - Wolf Creek Inn - Owned by Allen Family. Image from Clifton
Johnson's Highways and Byways

Au. 3_ We are staying at Mrs Allen's, such a nice, pretty place, and the family so clever. I feel like I was at home. A lady came yesterday with a little baby, and I never was so happy, as when Mother was nursing us both. I was anxious that every body should see us. Some time ago, Mother put a young baby in my lap, to see what I would do, and I commenced trying to cry like it, then laughed at it. The other day, I was stopped and sat down in Wolf Creek up to my neck, the first time I was ever in right cold water, but I am used to being bathed all over in water, a little warm. I can't begin to tell how delighted I was. I was splashing and kicking all the time, and doing my best to get away into deeper water. I could not take time to laugh outright, but was chuckling all the time, until I was taken out, when I always had a hearty cry. [BEGIN PAGE 12]

THE
WARM SPRINGS,

Madison County,

WESTERN NORTH CAROLINA.

HOWERTON & KLEIN, Proprietors.

HOT, WARM, TEPID AND COLD BATHS.

Readily accessible from every section of the United States, over
East Tennessee, Virginia and Georgia Railroad, and Connect-
ing lines of Rail, via Morristown and Wolf Creek, Tenn. ;
by North and South Carolina Systems of Railway,
via Salisbury, Charlotte, Spartanburg to Hen-
dersonville and Asheville, and by Fine
Coaches of the Western North
Carolina Stage Lines, to
Warm Springs.

Season EXCURSION TICKETS Sold on all Routes.

GREAT SOUTHERN SUMMER AND WINTER RESORT.

W. H. Ferrell, Book and Job Printer, Raleigh, N. C.

*Figure 25 - Ad for Warm Springs Hotel, c. 1880. Image from
https://docsouth.unc.edu/nc/howerton/howerton.html, accessed 26 Dec 2020*

Au. 8_ We left to day [*sic*] for the Warm Springs [*Scan QR code for short article about Warm Springs, modern day Hot Springs, NC*], eleven miles from here. The road is along the bank of the French Broad, all the way,_ some places it is so narrow there is barely room for a

carriage to pass, between the wall of rocks and the river. We passed right under the "Chimnies"_ immense towers 300 feet high. They are grand looking. A mile or so farther on, we

Figure 26 - Rock Art Visible at Paint Rock - Photo by Alex Stiner

passed the celebrated "paint Rock," [*Scan QR code for background info on Paint Rock*] with red painted marks on it, which have been there, as long as the oldest persons can remember. The hotel is situated on the other side of the river, from the road, and from the top of the hill, just before we get to the bridge, it does

look beautiful. We walked about a mile, before we came to the Hotel. Papa saw a horse and buggy fall off the bluff, once, and he was afraid for us to ride along it. It is a beautiful shady place, and if I could have got anything good to eat, I would have liked it very well. There is a fine warm bath here, but Mother did not put me in it, for fear I would take cold. One evening she put me in Spring Creek, it was much colder than Wolf Creek. There is music every day and night_ I have to go to bed so early, I never see the dancing. We staid [*sic*] ten days, and part of the time I was right sick. Pa cut my gums, and now I have another tooth. Uncle Jack, who was with us, staid [*sic*] two or three days, then went on higher up in the Mountains. He and Papa caught a good many fine fish. [BEGIN PAGE 13]

Au. 17_ We went back to Mrs. Allens to day [*sic*], where we expect to stay until cool weather. I am getting so fat staying here. I was not well fed at the Springs.

Au. 21_ This will always be a great day_ I walked to day [*sic*] by myself for the first time. I am so proud I can hardly take time for anything else, hardly to sleep. There is a little Spring about a quarter of a mile up Wolf Creek_ one evening I walked to it and back, and part of the time without any help. And if we came to a pretty sandy place, nothing could get me by, until I had a play in it. I walk every morning through Miss Emma's pretty flower garden, and bring in a handful of flowers for every body to smell. I crawl about so much at night, over the bed, Mother was afraid I might get a fall, so we have our bed put down on the floor. I commenced to have a frolic on it as soon as it was ready. I cry at night for my back to be rubbed with a hair glove. When in a good humour, I will mock myself crying. Father and Mother have picked out a pretty place, half a mile from here, on Wolf Creek, where we are going to have a Mountain home, and they have named it Glen_Ada. [BEGIN PAGE 14]

FIG. 15.—View of Peck Residence, Looking North.

Figure 27 - View of Glen Ada in 1893, from the Oblique City Prospectus. Text reads "Fig: 15—View of Peck Residence, Looking North". Original copy of prospectus owned by Betty Walker. Public Domain. Photo by the Editor.

Sep. 6_ We left Mrs. Allen's today, to go back to Oakland. Uncle Jack came a few days ago to go back with us_he brought us so many letters from Louisiana Grandpa and Grandma. We found all well when we reached home. Aunt Jane had come a few hours before us_ and Aunt Juliet was there too, and there were so many to handle and kiss me, that I had to take a good cry, before I could get acquainted again. I have so much fun running about their pretty yard. When Cousins Harry and I meet, we generally spend the day crying, time about, sometimes I try to be very friendly.

Oct. 6_ We left Oakland to day [*sic*], for Louisiana. We went in the carriage, and Aunt Patt_ Cousin Ellen_ and Uncle Jack went with us, as far as Loudon, which is a very pretty little place. In the evening, we

Figure 28 - 1889 Map of the Nashville, Chattanooga, and St. Louis Railway, and connections. Library of Congress. https://www.loc.gov/resource/g3701p.rr004720/, accessed 9 Jan 2021.

walked about a mile from town, to see the [*railroad*] cars pass. Instead of being frightened, I cried for them, after they went by.

Oct. 9_ This morning before day, we left Loudon in the [*railroad*] cars, and about ten o'clock at night, were in Nashville. It was a fine day for travelling. Part of the road looks very dangerous_ several miles of it, is on trussels, some of them seeming more than 150 feet high. When we went through the tunnel, I sat very still, with my arms round Mother's neck. It is about half a mile long, and [BEGIN PAGE 15] perfectly straight. When we were through, we could see the sun shining at the other end, which looked about as big as the full moon, when rising.

Figure 29 - Sign for Cumberland Mountain Tunnel, aka Cowan Tunnel, Photo by Ben Tate, March 2013. The East Tennessee and Georgia Railroad Co built 287 miles of railroad between Loudon and Knoxville in the years leading up to 1855. Ada and her family went through this tunnel within a year of its completion.

Figure 30 - Cumberland Mountain Tunnel, aka Cowan Tunnel, with train Q582 emerging from North end, Photo used with permission from Brent Michael, taken 11 Aug 2012.

Oct. 11_ We rested a day or so in Ashville. The river was so low there was no chance of getting a boat, so we concluded to leave in the stage, this evening, for Memphis.

Oct. 17_ We arrived in Memphis today. We had a dreadful trip through, for two days and nights, we travelled without stopping. I stood it very well. I soon learned to eat in a hurry, and was always glad when we could get out. Papa was taken very sick and we stopped at Jackson, where we staid [*sic*] three days, then we took a hack to Somerville [TN], and railroad from there to Memphis, where I got so little to eat, it made me very cross. We went out shopping_ it pleased me very much to walk along the street. I got some toys, and a rocking and table chair.

Oct. 21_ A little before day this morning, we landed at home, and off the steam boat Bulletin. We had quite a pleasant trip down_ there were a good many children on board, and I tried to get acquainted with them all. Mother told me so much about home_ I knew Grandpa and Grandma, as soon as I could get a good look [BEGIN PAGE 16] at them. What a busy day it has been _ so much to see, and so much riding in the fine little carriage.

SCAN ME

Nov. 8_ We all went to Uncle Bill's [*Scan QR code to learn about Brigadier General William Raine Peck, also see Appendix 9*] today_ he gave a grand dinner in honour of our return home. I did not behave very well, it was a strange place, and there were a good many strangers to speak to me, but at home, I am very good. I sit at the head of the table by Grandma, and behave like a lady. I can feed myself, and do not give any one much trouble. I call butter_ buccum_ and like it better than anything else. As soon as I have finished eating, I get down and bow awhile_ and then such a romp as I have running around the table. I like to have clean hands, and will hold them up high, until they are washed. I am sixteen months old, and am learning to talk very fast. I show the place where Papa whips me, when I am bad, which is very funny, after it is all over. I call Pa, Doccum, and have learned to scratch his head, which seems to do him a great deal of good. I have more toys and playthings, than I know what to do with. I am very good to stay in the house, when the weather is bad, _ if I know, I cannot get out, I do not fret, but try to amuse myself the best way, I can. I am a great mimic, trying to do every thing I see any one else do. I can sit like Lord Byron _ [*Scan QR code to learn more about Lord Byron*] and walk like Napoleon. I have [BEGIN PAGE 17] learned to say Uncle _ and when Uncle Bill comes to see us, I run as fast as I can, for my toys_ which stay under the bed_ to show

SCAN ME

him, for he seems to take great interest in them, which makes me more anxious to show all I have.

Figure 31 – Christmas Advertisement for Skerry's in Bangor, Maine. 25 Dec 1851 Bangor Daily Whig and Courier, Page 2. Shows Santa Claus about to go down a chimney. Text reads "Santa Claus! Santa Claus, annually brings On Christmas Eve, our pretty play things: A Ring for one, and a Toy for another—A Doll for me and a Drum for brother." "At Skerry's, No. 8 Main Street," "Head Quarters!"

Dec. 25_ This is Christmas day, and I am seventeen months old, too. Mother has been telling me, for a long time, that on Christmas Eve, she would hang a pair of my stockings, on the back of a chair, and that in the night, a little old fellow called Santa Claus_ would come, if I was a good girl, and put toys in them. I seemed to think, it would be a good idea to catch old Santa Claus, himself, for when Ma told me to be still and look for him, I would snap my fingers, and call "Tardels" (Carla). This morning I was helped out of bed, early, and holding my gown up, for it is too long, I ran to look in my stockings. Oh the pretty things in them. I brought them to the bed, for Pa and Ma to see_ holding my head, first on one side _ then the other, peeping in_ trying to make it out. I then sat down before the fire, on the floor to empty them_ in one I found a small_ very small_ tin tea set_ in the other I found such a pretty little bead bag, and a beautiful gold locket, with my name on the back, and Uncle Willie's likeness in the inside. I wonder how Santa Claus got it, to put in my stocking. This evening [BEGIN PAGE 18] I had a regular tea party_ had "sure enough" tea_ and set on a little table, that Mother played with, when she was a child. I had a wax candle in a pretty little silver candle stick, set in the middle of the table, and I sat up to it, in my rocking chair. I wanted, every few minutes, to put my finger in the candle. I expect it was a good thing I did not_ but it is hard. I can't have my own way. After I thought the Tea-party had lasted long enough_ with one jirk [*sic*] I cleaned off the table, when the tea-set was put away. My old nurse Mary, left me today for the first time_ she has gone to Vicksburg to see her Mother. I have been very good all day. [BEGIN PAGE 19]

Figure 32 - Ada's "Uncle Bill", William Raine Peck, source unknown, circa 1850

1855

Jan. 10_ Uncle Bill sent me so many pretty toys today_ a most perfect little farm, with trees_ cattle_ fowls_ and people_ and houses too_ and there is a funny looking, little figure, on a box with wheels, that, when I pull it, beats a drum with the legs_ and the hands hit together, two little brass plates. But the prettiest present of all, is a Parrot that can talk_I must quit crying or Polly will mock me. Oh what a great time I have had all day.

Figure 33 – Uncle Bill / "Big Peck," circa 1861, Courtesy of Jack and Kathy Spratt

Jan. 16_ A few days before we left Grandpa Peck's, Cousin Harry Rhoton and I, were measured. Our height, which was just the same_ thirty inches_ is marked on Grandma's room door. We heard today that he was dead_ he took the scarlet fever at Kingsport [TN], and died in twenty-four hours. Poor cousin Harry. He was a handsome little fellow, about two months older than I. [BEGIN PAGE 20]

Jan. 29_ At dinner, today, I called out for_ duck_a_day _ Apple_ and coppee (coffee)_ showing that I know what I want, and can ask for it. It is very cold now, and this is the first cold spell, this winter, that I have been perfectly well_ cold weather nearly always makes my gums hurt me. I am a year and half old now, and so very destructive. Of all the pretty toys that Uncle Bill brought me, not a month ago, I have hardly a perfect one, now. If I get tired of playing with them, down I throw them, as hard as I can. But the broken heads and feet, of men and animals, seem to suit me as well, as the most beautiful

Figure 34 - Children with Parrot by Christina Robertson in 1850,
https://www.mimimatthews.com/2015/07/09/the-pet-parrot-as-depicted-in-18th-and-
19th-century-art-literature-history/, accessed 26 Dec 2020

figures. On the 22ⁿᵈ, Grandpa and Grandma left home for New
Orleans, promising to bring me plenty of new toys. I have enough now,
to fill a small room.

Feb. 2_This has been a beautiful day, and I have been out of doors
nearly all the time. After dinner Mother took me on an old pony, and
went to the quarter to see the little niggums, as I call them. I went to

sleep, before we got there, but waked up to see them eating the apples and figs, we took to them. About half way home, I commenced calling for "dinny-dinny," and soon after was sound asleep, not waking up, till long after supper. About ten o'clock, Grandpa and Grandma came home, bringing me a little trunk and some pretty toys. One is a pretty [BEGIN PAGE 21] little Rafourt[?] on wheels that is wound up, and runs in a circle. I wonder how long I will keep them_ When Mother sees me sit down to examine any of them, that she wants me to keep, she puts them right away.

Feb. 14_ Papa shot some blackbirds today, and I ran as fast as I could to pick them up, dropping the dead ones, to catch those alive. I walked about the whole evening with my arms full, watching everybody, for fear some one, would take them from me.

Feb 20_ I weighed thirty pounds today, on a flatboat. A little girl off the boat came up to play with me, and I took great pleasure showing her all my toys, and dancing with her, while Mother played for us. We have such pretty dry weather now_ some evenings we go walking on the levee_ wane down_ as I call it, and play and roll on the grass.

Mar 4_ We took a long walk this evening down the levee, but I did not enjoy it, for I was sick. I am cutting my eye tooth, and it gives me a high fever. I have fallen off one pound. [BEGIN PAGE 22]

Mar. 11_ We went to see Uncle Bill today. I was very good. I believe the ride helped me, for I took a good nap, going and coming. Ma and Pa and Uncle left me and rode out to the "Mountain," as Uncle calls his place. Mary kept me amused, but sometimes I would miss them, and call loudly for Papee, I very often call him Pappay Peck.

Figure 35 - Crescent Plantation, Madison Parish, LA. Main section constructed in 1855.
One of the very few plantations in Madison Parish not burned during the Civil War.
Photo taken 1 Apr 2016 by Cookie Williams.
https://commons.wikimedia.org/wiki/File:Crescent_Plantation.jpg, accessed 4 Jan 2021.

Mar. 22_ This has been a most melancholy day for me. This morning Mother told me I must not ask any more for my "dinny," because I could not have it again. I understand what she said, and would pucker up my little mouth, when I looked towards it, but would not ask for it. I got through the day very well, for I was kept on the move all the time, but how I did miss it at night, although I did not cry much.

BURNING OF THE BULLETIN NO. 2.

*Figure 36 - Lloyd's Steamboat Directory: and Disasters On The Western Waters,
by James T. Lloyd, p 310, 1856, No copyright
https://digital.library.pitt.edu/islandora/object/pitt%3A31735054854082,
accessed 4 Jan 2021, see Appendix 4 for more info about Bulletin No. 2*

**The Steamers Bulletin and Huntsville De-
stroyed by Fire—Passengers Missing, &c.**
NEW-ORLEANS, Tuesday, March 27.

The steamer *Bulletin* was burnt on Saturday,
below Lake Providence, with 3,500 bales of cotton.
Twenty-three of the passengers and crew are mis-
sing. Among the former are J. B. WILLIAMS, of
New York, and Mr. McCAUSHE, of North-Carolina.
The lady passengers and the officers were all saved.
The vessel and cargo are a total loss. Boat in-
sured for $20,000.

The steamer *Huntsville* has also been destroyed
by fire, with 4,000 bales of cotton on board. We
have not yet learned the particulars.

The New York Times
Published: March 28, 1855
Copyright © The New York Times

Mar. 25_ Last night the river looked like it was on fire, which was burning cotton, and we heard this morning it was the Bulletin that burned [*See Appendix 4 for full account of Bulletin burning*], a few miles above us, the boat we came home on last fall. How fortunate for us she did not burn while we were on her, although she had some of our baggage and Ma's gun on board, that we left at Ashville last fall, to be sent to us. When ever any thing was said about the boat, I would say "poor peepee" for I understood it all, and a good many were burned, although it was early in the evening. [BEGIN PAGE 23]

April 3_ Last night while I was sound asleep, Father went out to kill some wild geese that were in a lot where we had two pet deer. The moon was shining very bright, and he was walking slowly towards the geese, when, as quick as lightning, without any warning, he was knocked down by one of the deer, coming up behind him. The deer was very mad and was trying to kill him. Pa got him by the horns and held him so fast he could not move, for about five long-very long minutes, screaming all the time as loud as he could, for some one to come. Grandpa hurried to him as soon as he heard him and pulled the deer off, being kicked down himself two or three times, but without being hurt much. He saved Father's life, for he could hold the deer no longer. He started to jump up to help Grandpa, when he fell back almost fainting, for his arm was broken, and he was cut and bruised all over. Grandpa had stabbed the deer several times, and he was pretty well worn out, when someone took the gun from under Papa, and shot him. Papa suffered a great deal getting to the house, for his arm could not be kept right still, but he had Grandpa and Uncle Willie[7] to help him, both strong.

Apr 29th_ Father has suffered so much with his arm, and it does not seem to be getting any better_ he left for New Orleans this evening, to see other doctors about it. My new nurse Rainey came up

---

[7] It is unclear whether this reference is to Ada's Uncle William Raine Peck who often goes by "Uncle Bill" or her Uncle Wiley Hawkins Peck, who also lived in Madison Parish. See Appendix 6 for the story when Wiley kills a man.

from Uncle Bill's today, so that I could get used to her before we leave home. I think I will like her very well. [BEGIN PAGE 24]

Figure 37 – Billy Buck of Henderson Plantation by Pattie Peck Harrelson, 2020.

May 6_ Last night about eleven oclock, Papa came home. I was asleep and he kissed without waking me, but soon after I waked, and as soon as I saw him, said, "pappy_pappy," and commenced climbing up to hug and kiss him. We talked a long time, I told him about Billy Buck_ and he told me, that he had found out his arm was broken, and never would be straight and strong again. I asked him about my gipsy hat, which he said he was going to bring me, and he did. I got so wide awake, it was some trouble to go to sleep again.

May 25_ I am 22 months old today, and am as smart, and as bad, as I can be. Grandma spoils me so much, she lets me do just as I please, and Mother scolds us both. I can sing parts of several songs, with lines of my own making_ Jim Crack Corn, is my favorite. Sometimes, when I am very good, I like to lie in bed and sing myself to sleep.

'2.

Den arter dinner massa sleep,
He bid dis niggar vigil keep;
An' when he gwine to shut his eye,
He tell me watch de blue tail fly.
    Jim crack corn &c.

3.

An' when he ride in de arternoon,
I foller wid a hickory broom;
De poney being berry shy,
When bitten by de blue tail fly.
    Jim crack corn &c.

4.

One day he rode aroun' de farm,
De flies so numerous dey did swarm;
One chance to bite 'im on the thigh,
De debble take dat blu tail fly.
    Jim crack corn &c.

5.

De poney run, he jump an' pitch,
An' tumble massa in de ditch;
He died, an' de jury wonder'd why
De verdic was de blue tail fly.
    Jim crack corn &c.

6.

Dey laid 'im under a 'simmon tree,
His epitaph am dar to see:
'Beneath dis stone I'm forced to lie,
All by de means ob de blue tail fly.
    Jim crack corn &c.

7.

Ole massa gone, now let 'im rest,
Dey say all tings am for de best;
I nebber forget till de day I die,
Ole massa an' dat blue tail fly.
    Jim crack corn &c.

771

Figure 38 - Jim Crack Corn, or, The blue tail fly. F. D. Benteen, Baltimore, monographic, 1846. Notated Music. https://www.loc.gov/item/sm1846.411670/. Info provided here for historical context; Neither the publisher nor the editor condones racism in any form. First Verse: "When I was young I us'd to wait On Mas_sa and hand him de plate; Pass down de bottle when he git dry, and bresh away de blue tail fly. Chorus: Jim crack corn I don't care, Jim crack corn I don't care, Jim crack corn I don't care, Ole Massa gone a__way."

Figure 39 - Steamboat Eclipse - Google Image

May 31_ We were ready today, to leave home, and hailed the fine boat Eclipse, but she would not stop for us. We are going to take the Parrot to Grandma Peck. [BEGIN PAGE 26]

June 2_ This has been like an October day_ A cold north wind has been blowing for two days. I have been very good today, after eating a hearty dinner, I went to sleep at the table, which made all laugh at me, but could not wake me.

Figure 40 – Steamboat Eclipse. Joseph M. Jones Steamboat Photograph Collection 1081, Series 8D, Box 2, Item 42, Louisiana Research Collection, Howard-Tilton Memorial Library, Tulane University.

June 4_ Yesterday Uncle William went to Vicksburg, to try to get the Niagara to stop for us, and today while all were at dinner but me, for I had gone to sleep at the table, she came in site, and commenced ringing her bell for us. Pa carried me on board, but I did not wake up till Ma put me in the berth, then she took me up to shake a handkerchief at Grandma_ Grandpa, and Uncle Willie, who were standing on the bank.

Figure 41 – Steamboat Rowena on the Cumberland River in 1907,
https://steamboats.com/museum/davet-photos3.html, accessed 26 Dec 2020

June 10_ We arrived at Nashville this morning, it was so pleasant we walked up to the Hotel. I was very pleased, for I ran after all the pigeons and chickens in my way, and called all the dogs I saw. We had a very pleasant trip up the river. We had no difficulty getting up the Cumberland river, although it was not very high. I went to the table today, and behaved very well.

June 11_ At eleven oclock last night we left Nashville in the [*railroad*] cars, and reached Knoxville this evening about 6 oclock, having come about 260 miles. I was so glad to get to a stopping place, we had a nice room at the Coleman House, and I danced about it, taking all sorts of fancy steps, to rest myself. As soon as it was dark Mother undressed me, and laid me down in bed myself, where I rolled about and sang, till I went to sleep.

June 12_ Early this evening we reached Oakland. Grandma and Aunt Jane were the only ones at home. I knew I had got home, and acted like I had only been away from it a week. I soon became acquainted, and when Grandma asked after Uncle Bill, I told her he was a bowlegged devil. Aunt Pattie came soon after us.

June 19_ Papa has been sick ever since we came, but yesterday feeling better, he and Uncle Jack started in the carriage, with nearly all our baggage, to Mrs Allen's. I miss him so much, my mouth puckers up, every time I say_ "Pappy is gone." Grandpa and Cousin Ellen McEffee came home the day after us. We went up to see Aunt Juliet a few days ago, I took quite a fancy to my cousins Jenny, Patty, and Emma, and we played together all day. Poor cousin Helen has been sick a long time, and she is still very sick, but Aunt thinks she is mending.

Polly Parrot was very tired of travelling, it was only a few days ago, that she commenced talking again. [BEGIN PAGE 27]

June 25_ When Poppa came home the other day he was most dead he was so sick, Uncle Doctor [*probably Dr. John F. Rhoton, married to Isham's sister Juliet N. Peck*] came at once to see him, gave him some medicine and got him warm, and in a short time he was a great deal better. Uncle Doctor vaccinated me that evening, and I sat perfectly still and saw him cut my arm and grip it, and as soon as he was done, I said he was a "bowlegged devil for cutting my honey baby's arm."

July 25_ I am two years old today, and as bad a child for any age as ever lived. I used to have a funny habit of, when I was mad, crying "spank me_ spank me" and falling flat on my face, when the spell would be over, but I have quit that now, and instead, cry a great deal more and bite my hands, clothes, and every thing near me, and get plenty of whippings for it, but I don't get any better. Nancy[*?* / *Possibly Nanny*] wore all the switches out that she had in her room, and this morning I was so bad she got a whalebone out of her trunk to whip me with, which being something new, I took it to play with and soon in good humour. We were going to have my birthday dinner up the creek, but it rained last night, and we could not go. Jane and Grandpa Hendy came about ten days ago to Mrs Allens. I knew them directly, and would go to no one else that [BEGIN PAGE 28] evening. Ma and Pa had walked up to Glen Ada, and though Jane was tired enough, she took me in the carriage and rode up there. We left Oakland as soon as Poppa was well enough, and have been here at Mrs Allen's almost a month. My arm made me right sick, but I was such a lady I never would scratch it.

[*End Of Journal*]

Ada Louise Peck
Born July 25, 1853 at "Oakland"
in Mossy Creek (now Jefferson City) Tennessee

Died March 25, 1858 at "Oakland"
Mother - Emma Henderson Peck
Father - Isham Talbott Peck

Quote from "my journal"
(written by her mother as though Ada wrote it)
dated August 21, 1854

"Father and Mother have picked out a pretty place,
half a mile from here, (the Allen Place) on Wolf Creek, where
we are going to have a mountain home,
and they have named it Glen Ada.

Figure 42 - Found on back of 1859 painting of Ada preserved at Glen Ada, printed in modern times, actual date of death is March 27, 1859. Actual location of death is Henderson Plantation in Carroll Parish, Louisiana. See Appendix 3 for letter from her mom describing the circumstances surrounding her death.

Figure 43 - Headstone for Ada Louise Peck, Peck section of Old Westview Cemetery, Jefferson City, TN. Photo taken by the editor 12 Jul 2017. Inscription reads, "ADA – DAUGHTER OF DR. I. T. & E. PECK. DIED MAR. 27, 1859, AGED 5 Y. 8 M.
"We are coming darling"

Emma's Letters

Emma Peck was a writer. She wrote Ada's Journal, but she also wrote letters to her friend Emma Allen in Wolf Creek, TN. She probably wrote much more than this, but they were not preserved as well as those contained here, which are found in the University of Tennessee Library in Knoxville. With few exceptions, all letters contained here come from the Wolf Creek Papers, MS.3858, Special Collections. "Emma's Letters" has two meanings. They are "Emma's Letters" because they were written by Emma Peck, but they are also "Emma's Letters" because most all of the letters contained here were written to Emaline "Emma" Allen (2 May 1821 – September 1888). Truthfully, they are more Emma Allen's than anything. Emma Peck wrote to her, Isham Peck wrote to her, Emma Peck's mom Louise wrote to her, and it was only once she died that people began writing to her relation Maggie Allen.

It is important to know that the Allen family ran THE place to stop in Wolf Creek, TN. I became aware of Peck family history intersecting with Allen history from Betty M. Walker, a descendant of the Allens, who still lives in Wolf Creek at the time of this writing. Here is an excerpt from an article she published called *Wolf Creek – An Old Stagecoach Inn Surrounded By Boxwoods* that speaks of both Emma Allen and where she lived.

> Reuben Allen came from Rockingham County, Virginia in the mid 1700s to a section of Tennessee now known as Cocke County. Reuben liked this mountain country. He built a log house, 90 by 40 feet, with four chimneys, a great porch, and a 'dog trot.' Mr. Allen went back to Virginia in 1805 and married Mary (Polly) Jones, a relative of Admiral Nelson. In the same year he brought his bride home to the Smokies of Tennessee.
>
> [. . .] Over the next twenty years ten children were born to Mary and Reuben Allen. Emma Allen, one of the young

daughters, was a natural artist. She designed the boxwood garden on the east side of the two-story house. Emma used the Mount Vernon Gardens for her model. She combined the common box for the borders with the dwarf box for the geometric designs. Emma used the common box on each side of the paths leading to the spring house, the barn, the school house and the cabins which housed guests when the 13-room house was filled. A single path led toward the railroad and the French Broad River and to the cemetery where today one finds the graves of Rueben Allen, his wife, several of Reuben's children and David Ward Allen, Reuben's nephew who became owner of the Allen home in the late 1800s. David's wife, Maggie, and their five children are also buried among the many boxwoods in the family cemetery.

[. . .] In 1867 when the East Tennessee, Virginia, and Georgia Railroad made its appearance, Wolf Creek was the terminal. The train stopped at Wolf Creek and passengers were taken by stagecoach to Hot Springs and Asheville, North Carolina. Many notable personages spent the night at Wolf Creek, including several United States presidents. By this time the old home had taken the name of The Allen Inn. Later it became known as the Wolf Creek Stagecoach Inn.

Betty goes on to share that such notable people as Woodrow Wilson eventually stayed at The Allen Inn. She also tells that the first post office in the area was in Wolf Creek and that the telegraph office was located at the Inn.

For more details on the Wolf Creek Stagecoach Inn and the Allen Family, please see the book *Sawbones: The Life and Times of Dr. Isham Talbot Peck* by Cross Mountain Books.

FIG. 1.—Allen Residence at Wolf Creek, Tennessee.

Figure 44 - Two images from the Oblique City, TN Prospectus of the American Oblique Manufacturing City Development Co, Incorporated 12 Jun 1893, Published by H. L. McQueen, Washington, D.C. Public Domain. Caption for Top Image: "Fig. 1—Allen Residence at Wolf Creek, Tennessee." Caption for Bottom Image: "Fig. 2—Flower Garden in Rear of Allen Residence."

FIG. 2.—Flower Garden in Rear of Allen Residence.

The letters contained here chronicle friendship, heartache, longing for connection, and also the intense feelings and opinions surrounding our nation's Civil War. Emma Peck grew up on one of the largest cotton plantations (Henderson) in Louisiana, with 143 slaves in 36 dwelling houses. Her views represented in her letters are typical of a southern woman of her time. Editorially, these letters are included to preserve family historical viewpoints, and do not represent the views of myself or Cross Mountain Books. Emma grew up just a short walk from Kate Stone, made famous by her journal *Brokenburn: The Journal of Kate Stone 1861-1868*. In *Brokenburn*, Kate shares of her experiences during the Civil War, including her connections with the Henderson and Peck families. She helps crochet the flag presented to Emma's brother-in-law, General William Raine Peck, when he is just a Captain and starting out; and she visits Emma's mom Louise after her husband, William Henderson, dies. She also spends a good deal of time with Louise's sister Minerva (Donohue) Prentice. Kate writes in 1867:

> "Mr. Rhotan and I became quite chummy when I went to stay a week or ten days with Mrs. Henderson after Mr. Henderson's death. We thought her so desolate and alone until her sister, Mrs. Prentice, came to stay with her—two lonely, elderly widows."[8]

Other books sharing first hand resources reflecting southern women's viewpoints during the Civil War include *Sanctified Trial: The Diary of Eliza Rhea Anderson Fain, a Confederate Woman in East Tennessee*, edited by John Fain and *A Very Violent Rebel: The Civil War Diary of Ellen Renshaw House*, edited by Daniel Sutherland.

---

[8] *Brokenburn: The Journal of Kate Stone 1861-1868,* Edited by John Q. Anderson, Louisiana State Univ Press, 1972, p 373.

Letters from Emma Peck to Emma Allen

December 21st 1854.

Dear Miss Emma

Doc answered your brother Green's letter not long ago. I am glad he has been so successful fishing. reading his letter made Doc wish he could have been with him. I hope next fall we will stay later. We did not leave Tennessee for a month after we left your house, and if we had waited for the river to rise, we might have been there yet. I am so glad we can have Glen Ada. You all know now it is no joke about our going back. I believe Wolf Creek and the mountains look prettier from down here, than when I could see them every day. I would like to see the Pines all covered with the snow. It is certainly the prettiest country in the world. Doc says please don't let anybody cut one of those beautiful evergreens, at Glen Ada, until he comes.

I would like for you if you could, to hire for me, some of your boys, to hunt and set out some of the wild Mountain Raspberry, opposite where the house will be. I will pay them when I come. There is a clump of White and Spruce pines across the road from where the house will be, that, if not too much trouble, I would like to have some cuttings of the [Page 2] Grape in your yard, put by them. I would have sent you some roses this winter, but Doc said a small bundle might get lost, and he thought the surest way for you to get them, would be when he made a shipment of fruit trees and shrubbery for our place. I send you some Arbor vita seed. I hope you will get them.

We have had a splendid fall and winter so far. Is the weather, in Tennessee, cool enough at last, for Mrs. Allen? I expect she feels like taking her breakfasts by a fire these mornings. I would like so much to see you all. Did Miss Cynthia get home without any adventures, and how did she leave her sister? Please write to me and tell me all the news. Mother sends her kind regards to you all, and she says she has heard me talk so much about you, you seem like old acquaintances. Ada is very well and fat, and never gets tired of running and dancing. How she will go next summer. She can say a few words right plain, and is a great pet with all. The little table cover you gave me, makes a spread of just the right size for her cradle. I have staid close at home this fall, and have been busy sewing all the time. I hope you have learned how to be lazy a little, I don't want you to be so industrious next summer, or you won't help to keep "that road warm." I hope this will find you all in good health. Give my love to Mrs Allen and Miss Cynthia. Your friend

Emma E. Peck.

[April 16, 1855]

Dear Miss Emma

I wrote to you some time ago, but not hearing from you, I begin to think that you did not get my letter, which had some Arbor vita seed in it, and for fear they are lost, I will take more to you. I send you in this some orange mater melon seed _ do not plant near any other kind or they will mix. We have real summer weather here, but it is so dry nothing grows well. We will have very little fruit here, I hope it is not the case in Tennessee.

I hope you are all well. I want to see you very much. I expect we will leave here about the first of June, Mother is going with us.

Ada is still very fat, and runs and talks all the time. Doc was very badly hurt by a pet deer, two weeks ago, he is just now beginning to get well. His shoulder was put out of place, and he was cut in several places. He would certainly have been killed in a very few minutes, but for Pa, who ran up and pulled the deer off him. Give my love to Mrs. Allen and Miss Cynthia, and believe me yours

Emma E. Peck

[*Louisiana*] Home Jan 2nd 1856.

My dear Emma

I would have written to you before now, but I knew Doc had written to Mr. Green about our trip home, and I have had nothing interesting to write until now, when I can tell you about my little Willy, a most remarkable boy _ we see already how very smart he is. You may know he is strong, by his starting to roll out of bed before he was three weeks old._ he is the very image of Pa, and is such a good child _ never cries. I never saw anything grow and fatten as he does. But I must not praise him too much, for fear you won't believe anything I say about him.   Ada is very good now, and thinks there is nobody like her little "budder." She very often asks after you all, and says she wants to see you.

How does Mrs Allen stand the cold this winter? We have had summer weather here, until ten days ago. The day before Christmas the yard was full of fine sweet roses. We have had a very little snow here, but I would like to be at your house now, and see it on the mountains, and Doc says we will after this, for he don't intend to leave Glen Ada, until the yellow fever disappears. It was dreadful, all along the river, last fall, worse at Milliken's Bend, for its size, than any place else, that I know of.

Is Mr Wash married yet? I thought the wedding was to have been [Page 2] some time last fall. Tell him for me, unless he is too busy writing love_letters, to please write to Mr Jones, to be sure to get any Maple Sugar for me. And tell him, when he writes, not to forget, and direct it to Cleveland. Tell Mr Green the Swamp is full of Deer, but

Doc has not been hunting anything but Wild Cats?. If he had come down, I expect they would have had plenty of sport. Have you had a merry Christmas? the weather has been too bad here, to think of fun. Ada had the most fun looking at the new toys old father "Nickolas" brought her.

Do you and Miss Cynthia ever take time to go to Glen Ada? The house must be pretty near done by this time. Whenever a cold spell comes, you don't know how I regret, that we could not get an sec[ond]? house built. Don't treat me as you did last winter, but write as soon as you get this. I want to hear from you all. Tell Mr Green to write often. I heard Doc wishing to night, he could get a letter from him.

Give my love to Mrs Allen _ Miss Cynthia and Martha. Yours truly

Emma E. Peck

I heard Doc speak of some very white flour he saw at Swaggertys, tell Mr Green if he should be at Mr James Allen's before we go up, to please try to engage some of it for me.

Home Decem 6th 1856

To Dear Ema Emma G Allen
Dear Emma S? Emma I thought [*sic*]

I thought you would like to hear how we all are, this morning, and that maybe I could get you to write a few lines back to me. We have been here about ten days, had a very long, unpleasant trip, we were all sick with colds, and the children tired of traveling, and very bad, and to crown all, landed from the boat in the hardest kind of a rain. We staid one day at Oakland, all were well. Willy has been very sick since we came home, has a large rising on his neck, Doc lanced it yesterday. Mother is very well, the place looks very pretty, there are a few roses in bloom yet, Doc paid a man in Nashville, to send a large bundle of fire roses up to the mountains in April, I hope they will go safe. He is much obliged to Mr Green for forwarding the letter to him. We saw Mr. Wash in Knoxville, and looked out for him [*the*] next day, but did not see him, I thought it likely he had followed Miss "Cleveland" [*to?*] Georgia. Mother sends her love to you all. Give my love [to] Mrs Allen and Miss Cynthia, and do write soon.

Yours affectionately

Em[ma E. Peck.]

Home Oct. 28th 1857

Dear Miss Em

I don't believe you will answer this letter, and let me know how you all come on, and as I told you, I won't look for any. We have been here two weeks _ had a safe, but not very pleasant trip home _ the [*railroad*] cars and boat were too much crowded, and the weather pretty warm. Ada and Willy caught cold on the boat and have been quite sick ever since_ Willey is almost right well now, and I hope Ada soon will be. May and Pa are very well_ Pa took the chill and fever after he got home and was very sick for awhile. We found all well at Father's _one of Dr. Rhoton's daughters had typhoid fever_ She had been very sickly in Jefferson. The sugar cane mill worked beautifully, and I am sure that if Mr Wash could see how comfortably the person sits, that passes the cane through, he could go right to work to build a mill, so he could have that job to do. There has been no frost or cold weather here yet. The yard is full of such beautiful roses, I do wish you could see them. It is such a pity they won't grow as well with you.

Ask Mr Green if we must look for him to eat Christmas dinner with us.   I asked Ada what word she wanted to send to you, and she says _ "tell Miss Em the birds sing so pretty here".   Mother says she is going to write to you soon [Page 2] Give my love to Mrs.

Allen and Miss Cynthia, and tell her I will think her right mean if she gets married without letting me know. Now don't forget_ be sure not to write me a line.   Yours affectionately

Emma E. Peck

Home Decem 28th 1858.

Dear Miss Emma
                    I hope you are all well. and have had a merry Christmas, I looked a little for Mr Wash or Mr Green to take Christmas dinner with us, but were disappointed again.   We had a very pleasant trip home, and all were well, and found Pa and Ma well we staid so long at Oakland, they were getting uneasy about us [.] Willy and Charley have been very sick since we came home, but are quite well now, Ada has not been well for a week, but has not been sick enough to take medicine, she seems a little better to day, and I am in hopes the spell will soon wear off.   When she and Willy are talking of anything that pleased them very much they always tell of the time they went around the lot in the buggy, when you were in with them _ that was fun.   Mr. Wash helped us along so much, the day we left your house, did he tell you about the trouble we had, to keep Willy from going back home with him _ we drove into Greenville just at sundown, I like that road so much better than the others to Oakland, we found [?] [?] there, but have not heard from there since we left. I hope you have had better weather than we have had, it has been windy _ rainy and foggy all the time, I think I have seen the sun twice since I came home, but I won't be certain and the mud is so deep I can't get out of the yard. The river is very high and rising, I am very much afraid there will be another overflow.   I have not a word of news to

tell you, I hope you got the tea_pot for Mrs. [?], I wish she had let me [?] sooner that she wanted it. Give my love to her and Miss Cynthia, I would like to [hear] from you, but be sure not to answer this letter.

Your friend
Emma E. Peck.

Give my love to Miss Martha, and tell her not to stay in the house too much, this winter[9]

Oakland April 22nd 1859

My dear Miss Emma

I ought to have written long ago, but I could not. Have you heard that my dear darling Ada is dead _ she was sick only a few hours, and died on the 27th of March, at 8 o'clock in the morning _ O it was so hard to give her up _ she had grown to be the best dearest little darling that ever was _ She never seemed so well and bright as she did; the morning of the day she was taken sick, and about the middle of the day was suddenly taken with Cholera Morbus,[10] we gave her some simple remedies, and thought she was better, but a fever came on at dark which lasted till next morning, when she died, so peacefully and without a pain _ we could not get a doctor there till it was too late, and he said he could not have done her any good, that she had Conjestion [sic] of the Brain, and he tell us now, that he has been watching darling for a [Page 2] long time, and knew we could not keep her with us. After she was dressed we kept her three days, she looked perfectly beautiful, I put fresh flowers round her every

---

[9] Copy of this 1858 letter given to editor by Ann Kirkpatrick Peck
[10] See Appendix 5 for more info about the cholera epidemic in the mid-1800s

morning _ we have here a perfect likeness of her, that we had painted_ it looks like she was sleeping. She is in a beautiful metallic case, with a glass top, so we can look at her again, she is here with us, a vault is built in the yard here above ground, to put her in _ you don't know how broke up and lost we feel. After losing her down in that dreadful country [*East Carroll Parish, Louisiana*], we got uneasy about our other children, and left home sooner than we expected _ I am not going back with them any more. I would like so much to see you, can't you come here, we are not going up to Glen Ada this summer, but I want to go and stay awhile at your house, some time this summer, Father here, told me when I wrote to you that I must beg you to come, and to be sure and make Mrs. Allen come with you, I wish you would, I want to see you both so much, I have so much to talk about my darling. Give my love to Mrs. Allen[,] Miss Martha & Miss Cynthia. Your affectionate friend

Emma E. Peck

Oakland July 1st 1859.

Dear Miss Emma

                      I was beginning to wonder if you could have received our letters, and why you did not write, when a letter from Mr Wash came telling us you were all well, which I was very glad to hear.   Mother is here now, she came up with Aunt Minerva and Uncle Prentice, who are at Greenville. Pa will not be up before the first of August, he was very well when I last heard from him. Poor Cousin Horace had typhoid fever, he was sick about a week, Aunt did not hear of his being sick, until she heard he was dead_ what a shock it was. Mother sends her love to you all, and says she expects to see you some time this summer. Willy says I must tell you that he has a pretty little skiff, which he is going to learn to pull_ he and Charley have not been very well for two or three days_ all the rest of us are well. [Page 2] and send love to you Mrs Allen and Miss Martha. My new room is finished and it is very comfortable, you left your comb here, I will send it to you by the first opportunity_ I am sorry I did not think to send it by Mr Ware?. You must write soon to

Yours truly Emma E. Peck

Doc says please ask Mr Wash to pay his taxes for him

[*Written on page 3 of the above 1 Jul 1859 letter is the following letter from Emma Allen to Emma Peck, numerous misspellings are preserved*]

Home July the 10th [18]59

My Dear friend M

It has

Seemingly quite @ serious time since I seen or heard from you but by thee law of reverence I am keeping my promis so far as the writing part is concerned I intend that you shal see that I have left it as part of my pledge will be concealed from you until the affixed time rowls round when I am to make a full confession and I hope that I can make perfectley true one so that you will see that I have lived according to promis I haven't anything that is worth communicating but what I have I think will serve to rouse you from one of your deep reveries   Emma, Gantry, Allen

Allen Castle Tennessee

Figure 45 - https://www.findagrave.com/memorial/53256470, accessed 3 May 2020, Florence Cemetery, Lauderdale County, AL Plot P3-09. Inscription reads: "Horace Prentice Jr. Only Son of Horace & Minerva S. Prentice BORN in Lake Providence, LA. Dec. 28, 1838 DIED April 3, 1859

Oakland July 6th 1859

My dear Miss Emma

John starts in the morning to bring me some of my things from Glen Ada, Doc was going too, but he has not been very well lately, so he put off going yet awhile. I send you a list of what I want, and as you know where every thing is, I hope I am not troubling you too much in asking you to have them sent to me.   Please send me Darling's little dresses, and her little flower pot that is on the mantle piece in my room, and please send me her little dog.   I think the glass globe of the lamp will come safe by putting it between two pillows, and rolling some of the other things round them_ the glass Chimneys can be rolled in the same way_ you will find them and the wicks in a box, on the shelf in the pantry that is opposite the door.   I don't want the keg of vinegar now, we have some_ Doc says he thinks Aaron knows where the closet is undern[eath] the kitchen. The Tobacco is in a bag hanging up in the pantry. [Page 2] The bed clothes and towels are on a shelf in the bath room. There is flat box of toilet soap in the pantry, if you can find it please send me about half of the soap.

I wish I could see you all, but I don't think I can get up this summer_ be sure to write to me by John and let me know when you are coming to see me again. We are all well, and I hope so are you. Give my love to Mrs Allen and Miss Martha. Yours truly

Emma E. Peck.

Oakland Dec 4th 1859

My dear Miss Emma

I have been looking for you so long, I begin to think now you have no idea of coming to see me, and you know too, how much I would like to see you. Doc wrote to Mrs

Allen that I had another little boy, did she get the letter. [?] I call him Edward, he is seven weeks old, and a mighty good little fellow, I am glad he is, for having no regular nurse, I have to nurse him a great deal. Mother came up to see us when he was two weeks old. and staid a few days, she thought I was very sick and left home in a hurry. she says Aunt Minerva and Lelia got home safe and well. If Mrs Allen received Doc's letter, you heard how sick [*Isham's brother*] William [*Raine Peck*] was here, and how near he came dying, he staid until quite well before going home, and then Albert Rhoton went with him, he is learning engineering from Wiley [*Hawkins Peck*]. All were well [Page 2] when I last heard from home. I am looking every day for my Piano and some of my Darling's toys from home. One of the spruce pines you sent me is green yet, and I am in hopes it will grow. I hope I can soon get her little sofa and al her little things from Glen Ada, so I can have them all together. I never saw Willy and Charley so fat and healthy as they are now_ Charley is a great imprudent looking fellow_ calls out "good morning" to strangers that pass him in the road, and has a funny way of saying bad words. He waked up soon one morning, and the first thing he said was_ "I want to see Mrs Allen". I asked him what I must tell you for him, and he said "something pretty". Mother, Father and all are well_ Sister Jane came down while William was sick, and staid until two or three weeks ago, she was well when she wrote last. Mr and Mrs Swett staid here three or four days after they came from the Mountains_ they were so much pleased with you all. I hope you will be down soon, but please answer this, I want to hear what you are doing. [Page 3]

Is Mr Wash married yet, he ought to let Doc know how he comes on courting. Tell Mrs Allen that Doc does not do much else but settle church difficulties, she would suppose, to hear him, that he was one of the main props of the church. He is taking depositions, and says he can't get ready with some of the cases till next fall. I hope you are all well, give my love to Mrs Allen, Miss Cynthia and Miss Martha, Remember me to Mr Wash and Mr Green. Yours truly

Emma E. Peck

[P.S.] Mrs Swett was very careful of the boquet [*sic*] you sent one_ you don't [*know*] how glad I was to get it. Please save me some of the Dahlias, so I can try to get them here next year. I want you to have those two rose bushes in the garden, now is a good time to move them to your garden, if you think they would do better. Mrs Swett told me, when she gave me your letter that you talked of coming down with Aunt Minerva_ I have been looking for you ever since.

Oakland Feb 15th 1860

Dear Miss Emma

I received your letter a week since, I am so sorry to hear you have been sick, you ought to have paid me that promised visit, it might have helped you, and you know we wanted to see you, and you have to take that ride on the [*railroad*] cars yet. I am glad Mrs Allen keeps well, but I think this has been a right cold winter for her, after having our sick spell, we have been perfectly well, the children have run out of doors all the time, Willy took great pleasure in tramping through the snow.   Doc got back from New Orleans a week ago, came all the way on the railroad_ he left New Orleans on Saturday night and was [Page 2] here Tuesday morning, a quick trip, but it can be made very easily in forty_eight hours. I think he wrote all about Wiley's difficulty, to Mr Wash_ as soon as he heard of it, he started down, and staid until Wiley was acquitted. He killed a mean man, but had to do it in the self_defense.[11] I hear pretty regularly from Pa and Ma, I got a letter two or three days ago, they were well. Don't be so long answering this letter, I want to hear from you oftener. Willy said I must not send this off, without letting him write some to you.   Edward is the best little fellow I ever saw, and it looks like it was going to last_ I was going to say, I thought it had been a month since he cried any, but I remember that to night while Jenny was undressing him, he did cry some_ just enough to let us know he knew how. I wish [Page 3] Charley was half as good as he is. Sister Jenny was here a few days ago, she was very well. Father, Mother Sister Matt [*Martha A.F. Peck*] and all are well. Doc has not quite got over his fatigue and cold yet. Give my love to Mrs Allen, My respects to Mr Wash and Mr Green.

Your friend

Emma E. Peck

[P.S.]   I don't know whether this receipt is of any account or not, it seems simple enough. Fourteen or fifteen nettle seeds ground into powder, and taken daily, will cure the swelling in the neck known by the name of goitre, without in any way injuring the general habit.

Oakland June 16th 1860

Dear Miss Emma

Thank you for sending the Dahlia roots and verbena, they came very quick, but Doc was so sick I could not put them out as soon as I wanted, but some of the verbena is growing, and all the dahlias. Please save me some seed of the Portilacca. Did you get some cantelope seed that I sent you in a letter. [?]

---

[11] See Appendix 6 for an account of the killing of Charles N. Harris by Emma's brother-in-law Wiley Hawins Peck in self-defense

Willy and Charley have been a little sick a day or two, the rest of us are well. About a week ago Doc was taken sick like the spell he had in the Mountains, and came very near dying, but we treated him differently and he was not sick near so long. [Page 2]

I think it likely our mountain house will be occupied this summer, Mr Brown of New Orleans has just written to know how to get there. I received a letter from Mother the other day, all well. I was sorry to hear Mrs Allen has not been well. I would like to see her, and hope she is quite well again by this time. Give my love to her, write soon and let me know how you are all getting on. Yours truly

Emma E. Peck

[P.S.] Doc says please ask Mr Wash to pay his taxes, and that he is going to try to get up to see him.

If Mr & Mrs Brown do come to our house, will you please be so kind as to pack in a box our wearing things that we left there (I can hardly remember what they are, but I know I left some few things), you know they will use every thing that belongs to the house, and I did not want anything left in the drawers.

Oakland Nov 27th 1860.

Dear Miss Emma

You won't come to see me and you won't write. that comes of being in the church, I knew it would do you harm. I can't tell how disappointed I feel. That I could not get up to see you this fall, and I do want to see you and Mrs Allen so much. We have been right busy trying to get fixed for winter, I am keeping house now, Sister Matt, Mother[*Sophia W. (Talbott) Peck*] and Father [*Judge Jacob F. Peck*] moved to their new house two months ago, and I have had so much to do I could not get off to see you. We are all pretty well, you would hardly know Willy and Charley, they have grown so. Edward is not near so large as Charley was at his age. I wish you could see him. Willy is learning to read and write so fast, I think he can soon write you a letter, and Charley spells remarkably well without knowing a letter. I heard from Mother [*Louise (Donohue) Henderson*] and Father [*William Henderson*] a few days ago, both were well. [Page 2] Aunt Minerva did not go home with them. We heard it was sickly where she lived, Mother was afraid for her to take Lelia home, and wrote to her about it. I thank you so much for all the things you sent me, and would have written my thanks before now, but kept hoping to see you. I think every thing will grow. The Dahlias were late, but most of them bloomed very pretty. Mother wrote that Mr and Mrs Brown arrived safely at home, both very much improved. How is Miss Cynthia and Miss Martha, do write soon and tell me what you are doing. When the railroad is finished, I will feel like running up to see you every week. I hope this will find you all well. Yours Truly

Emma E. Peck

Oakland Feb 12th 1861.

My Dear Miss Emma

I have not had much to tell you, or I would have answered your letter sooner, I will be glad when the time comes for you to pay me that visit, talking to you will be better than writing. I am all the time busy about something, this pretty weather I have been gardening some, I won't tell what I have done, for I expect you are far ahead of me. I don't think this winter has been near so pleasant as last was, the awful rains have kept us shut up nearly all the time. We had fun while the snow lasted, Willy and I worked so hard rolling snow balls. I don't think I ever saw such a deep snow before [Page 2] or so beautiful as it was. How I would love to see our Mountain place [*Glen*

Ada] covered with snow. The children have kept very well all winter, Willy spends most of his time writing letters to Pa and Ma. I heard from them to day, both very well, I suppose you have heard by this time, that being in Louisiana, they do not live in the United States now, I wish I could say the same thing of myself. I don't think a woman has any business talking politics, but I hear what is going on, and it looks to me like it was the interest of this state to go right along with the South. Doc says he can't hear of a man here, that ever sold anything to the North, but I think they have all voted to stay with it. We heard to day that Jeff Davis has been elected Southern President. Tell Mrs Allen I think [Page 3] Edward is prettier than the other boys, he can run everywhere now, and Willy and Charley have a great time watching him. Write soon and tell me when you are coming, and try to get Mrs Allen to come too, I want to see her so much. Yours Truly

Emma E. Peck

[*P.S. in Child's Handwriting*]
Dear Miss Emma I want to see you very much.
Will Henderson Peck

[*Letter inserted here from Mrs. Brown of New Orleans. The Browns stayed at Glen Ada during the summer of 1860 as listed above*]

New Orleans
April 16, 1861

Dear Miss Emma

Your kind and welcome letter of the 6th of April was received yesterday, and I am glad to hear you all are well, and that the long and disagreeable winter is past and that spring has let in. Yesterday is the first time I have had a letter from you, I presume the reason I did not receive the first, was because you did not inspect to the case of some one as I never scarcely receive a letter unless directed to the case of "Rotchford Brown Geo" on the case of "Brown and Johnstone" either will answer. Brown being such a common name I never have letters even enquired for, unless directed to some firm. We have had spring weather here for a long time past; everything looking very beautiful; and flowers in perfection at this time.

[Page 2] You ask me if we expect to be in the mountains during the next summer; I am sorry to say I don't expect to leave New Orleans during this year; we are in too much trouble to think of anything but defending our country to the last; very little is thought or talked of except war; we are out of the Union and no one ever dreamed of ever returning, the die is cast for the South; she will never return, no hope of that.[12]

I hope your mother's health has improved, you mentioned how thin she became "is it going to ill health; I trust not.

---

[12] The State of Louisiana declared that it seceded from the United States on 26 Jan 1861. It then announced that it had joined the Confederate States. Louisiana was the sixth slave state to declare that it had seceded from the U.S. and join the C.S. (Source: Wikipedia, accessed 16 Feb 2021)

I shall never go to the mountains any where near you all without going to see you; I often revert to the pleasant time I passed in the mountains [*at Glen Ada*], and to the great kindness I received from every member of your family one and all; and hope to see you all again; but when that will be [?] now can from no idea_ [?] trust the affairs of our country [?] will be settled in a few months.

[Page 3] Mr. Brown's health has improved since last fall, altho he is still far from strong, and never uses either, tea or coffee as well as, he loved both, he lives chiefly on milk, cracked wheat and cold bread, and occasionally a little fresh meat, beef or mutton. If I live during the summer, how often my thoughts will return to the cool mountain air, and pleasant [?] I enjoyed last summer.

My Mother had been very feeble all the past winter, sick very often. You all must have missed Miss Mattie during the long winter, give my love to her when she returns home.

"How is your Brother Green's health?" I hope he is entirely relieved of his dyspepsy.   I have a few flowers, but they are far short of what I saw in your garden; it is very difficult to grow small annual flowers with us; the hot sun and insects are a great preventative; I sometimes become discouraged.

Mr Henderson has been in the [Page 4] once or twice; but Mrs Henderson has not, he said she was well & that they intended going to visit Mrs [*Emma E.*] Peck in the summer.

Say to your Brother, that Mr Brown intends sending the gun the first person he meets with going to Greenville.   Give my kind love to your Mother and kind respect to both your Brothers also to Mr Wash Harris_ Mr Brown sends kind regards to you all_ Let me hear from you soon.

Yours truly and affectionately
Louisa N. Brown.

Figure 46 - Gen Turner Ashby, CSA in the 18 Oct 1862 Southern Illustrated News

[Oakland ~Summer/Fall 1862]

My Dear Miss Emma

I have just received your letter, if I cannot get to see you, I wish I could hear oftener from you, but for the war we would have gone to see you long ago. I don't think the war will last much longer, and as soon as it is over we will be up, I have so much to say to Mrs Allen and all of you. My boys keep very well and grow so fast, Willey rides his little pony for the mail now. Charley is nearly as large as Willy. Eddy says he knows you very well. We have named the baby for the Hero Genl Ashby[13], who was killed in Virginia. He is a great big good natured fellow, and not as pretty as the other children, I have no nurse for him, so I am kept pretty busy. It is a long time since I heard from home, Pa and Ma were going to stay at home and try to take care of their property [*Henderson Plantation*]. Vicksburg, which is making such a brave stand [Page 2] is only forty miles below our place. The whole country was overflowed, and it has been several months since Mother had heard from Aunt Minerva. The river is falling very fast now. I am much obliged to you for taking care of my things. I would like for you to take the rest of the silver and anything else you could find room for, but I hope you won't trouble too much about it. I am glad Mrs Allen keeps well, give my love to her, Miss Cynthia and Miss Martha. Try to come to see us soon. I hope you are all well.

Yours Truly

Emma E. Peck

Oakland April 1st 1866

I don't know whether you will get this letter. I will start it from here, by Father [Judge Jacob Peck], who is going to his silver mine, and thought it possible he might have a chance of sending it to you. I received a letter from you last summer, but have had no way of sending an answer. Is there a mail to the Warm Springs yet? I will be glad when there is, for I would like to hear from you often. Father [*Judge Jacob Peck*] saw Miss Cynthia last December, I believe, who told him she was coming to see us soon and I have been looking for her every day since, I wish she or you would make haste and come. [Page 2] We have all

---

[13] Profile for Gen Ashby can be found here: https://www.shenandoahatwar.org/history/turner-ashby/, accessed 1 May 2020

kept very well this winter but Doctor, he has suffered a great deal with rheumatism, this climate is too cold for him, I think we will have to move away to a warm one. I wish you could see my house_ ful of boys. Will is nearly as tall as I am, and Charley nearly as large as he is. and there is not much difference between Eddy and Ashby. There is another you don't know_ Louis, who will be a year old in May. You would have more fun with our old bad Ed, than any of them I don't know what would have become of us without his badness. I hear from Pa and Ma pretty often, she says Pa [*William Henderson*] looks badly, he had a severe spell of sickness last summer, and has not been right [Page 3] well since_ they have rented the plantation this year. Aunt Minerva has come back from Texas, she was well. Brother Wiley is dead. He came from Texas in September, and was living at our house. One morning in January he rode down to see William, and while talking to him, was taken suddenly with hemorrhage of the Lungs, and died in about an hour. It was a hard blow to Mother and Sister Matt. You may have heard that brother William has been pardoned.[14] He passed down on the train New Year's day, but we did not get to see him. Sister Jane was well when we last heard from her. She came down [*from Kingsport, TN*] last August and staid [Page 4] nearly five months, and we were all so sorry when she went home. We are trying to garden on a new plan this year_ we allow the chickens to pulverize the ground, and notice that the seeds come up a great deal quicker. The fact is, we have no way to keep them out, we think so much of our chickens, having been without any for so long, that we are waiting to see which will get the best of the fight. How do you come on raising chickens_ I have over fifty young ones. We have our fields fenced in once more, they are rented, and it begins to look like living to see the plows running again. Doc says please make up the blankets, sheets[,] pillow cases and towels in a bundle, and the first chance [Page 5] get Mr. Wash to send them

---

[14] See Appendix 9 for more info about Gen William Peck's Presidential Pardon

to some merchant in Greenville with directions to forward them to him by Express [.] We get on very well with our cooking, each one cooks his dinner to suit himself, and about once in twenty_four hours I get the dishes washed up. How you would laugh to see us. I almost forgot to thank you for the dress pattern you wrote about, Mother sent me a dress, but if you don't want it, it would make shirts for the boys. I hope you are all well. Give my love to Miss Cynthia please remember me to Mr Wash and Mr Green.

Yours truly

Emma E. Peck.

Oakland Sep 17th 1866

My Dear Miss Emma

Will is so glad because he is going to the mountains with John_ I wish we were all going_ and I hope he will find you all well. They will bring the blankets, and if they can be packed better to curl them in two, please do it_ and please send the towels_ red table cover and spoons. I wanted one of my spreads but I don't expect they could bring it. You must write to me by Will if you get home safe and [Page 2] how your doves are doing, and if Mr Green found all right at his place, and when you are coming again. Give my love to Miss Cynthia and Miss Martha and my respects to Mr Wash and Mr Green.

Yours truly

Emma E. Peck

P.S. I have heard lately from Mother, she has been sick and I am looking for her up sometime this fall. I expect William will be up too. We are looking for sister Jane [*(Peck) McEffee / Lynn*] tomorrow or next day.

Oakland Nov 24th 1867

My Dear Miss Em

        I intended writing by Father [*Judge Jacob Peck*] when he went to Newport, but he started sooner, than I expected, and now Mr Baughman is going there, and I will send this by him, in hopes he will see some of you_ if you should see him, be sure to send me a letter. I hear sometimes that you are well but I wish you would write to me. Doctor is still in Louisiana I expect he will be at home by the end of the year. The [Mississippi] river fell too late for him to make a good crop_ very few have good crops_ William's is good. They, and Mother and [Page 2] Aunt Minerva are well, but it has been a terrible year for sickness_ about half of the people have died_ and there never was any thing like the way the negroes have died of Cholera, a good many died on our place, and 83 died on one place near Milliken's Bend.[15] Every body wants to leave that dreadful country_one man sold his place for 50 cents an acre and left for Honduras_ another offered his well improved place for one dollar an acre, and could not get it. You never heard of such distress in your life, as in poor Louisiana this year. I have just received a letter from Mother_ she says it is the first time she ever wanted to leave there.   I am glad to hear they are getting on so finely with the railroad_ I am in hopes we will get up to see you next summer, and if we don't, you must be sure to come see us [.] Mother staid with me from April until September. Write me a

---

[15] See Appendix 5 and also historical notes regarding cholera pandemic here: https://en.wikipedia.org/wiki/1863%E2%80%931875_cholera_pandemic where it says, "Outbreaks in North America in the 1870s killed some 50,000 Americans as cholera spread from New Orleans via passengers along the Mississippi River and to ports on its tributaries." Quoting: Beardsley GW (2000). "The 1832 Cholera Epidemic in New York State: 19th Century Responses to Cholerae Vibrio (part 2)". The Early America Review. 3 (2). Retrieved 2010-02-01. https://www.varsitytutors.com/earlyamerica/early-america-review/volume-4/the-1832-cholera-epidemic-part-2, accessed 1 May 2020

long letter and tell me all about how you are getting on. Give my love to Miss Cynthia, and tell her I am still looking for her_ she might very well come over with her step son, when he comes to New Market to school, and stay a week or more with me. Give my respects to Mr Wash and Mr Green and Wife.

Yours truly
Emma E. Peck.

Figure 47 - Painting of Judge Jacob Peck, oil on fabric, c. 1830, by Ralph E. W. Earl. East Tennessee Historical Society Collection, gift of Martha Rogers Withers, photo by Editor 12 Jul 2017

Letters from Isham Peck to Emma Allen

[Oct 1856]

Miss Emma

  I send you seed of the Chinese Sugar Cane _ so call'd in the letter in which I recieved (sic) it from the patent office_

  Cultivate like broom corn _ either in drill or in hills _ It is in fact a <u>corn</u> – <u>but</u> very sweet _ & will make sugar or molasses _ I have no doubt of its value _ The dry season they cut short my seed, or you should have had more _ But the most you can do is ta (sic) get seed for next year _

  Plant it about the time of early corn protruding? In good ground 40? _

  Send you also the Japanese pea _ used as the Black eye p[ea] _

  Drop seed one or two to the foot in the row _ it grows as a bush_

Respectfully

Oct 1856   T Peck

[On the back of one of the letters and undated]
Your brother has seen and tasted the stock. but I think I can see he will take no interest in it_ or copper _ harmful [?]!! I rely on you_that's it.

May 8th [No Year Listed, but after 1859]

Dear Miss Emma

  My darling Ada told one when I went to New Orleans, to be sure to buy her a present for that good Miss Emma, After she died I was in N[ew] Orleans and I remembered what she said, I bought you a dress _ Which we would have tried to send to you, but we have been hoping that you would come to see us_ I am trying to build some rooms here, but the people are so much troubled with religion and politics that I find it very difficult to get any thing done. I think I have two summer coats at Glen Ada [,] one black and one linen one, my wife says they are in a drawer in the bath room. will you please to make a bundle of them. And I will try to get the Mail Carrier to bring them to me _ Love to all the family Respectfully your friend

I. T. Peck

Oct 18th [18]59

Mrs [*Mary "Polly" (Jones)*] Allen
Dear Madam

Emma has another little boy [*Ed*], now three days old_ mother and child doing very well_ The other boys grow very fast _ Charles is tall _ most as large as William, and is the smartest child I ever saw_ I cannot write or speak of my dear last child [*Ada*] [.]

My brother William came here about five weeks since, he was very sick and for many days, we had little hope of recovery, He left here for home yesterday in perfect health. We want to see you all_ but for Emma helpless condition we would have visited you this fall_ I have been very busy, building some rooms, and nursing my brother the last month _ Miss Emma promised to come to see

[I. T. Peck]

Letters from Louise Henderson to Emma Allen

January 2nd [1856]

My Dear Emma

A happy new year to you and to each and every individual of the family.

I would have written to you before this, but I have felt so little like writing. I had been home but a few days when I heard the melancholy news of my dear nephew's health, and I have felt badly enough. It seems as if I must pay a penalty if I am every happy, last summer I was happy as the ages were long, and I anticipate so much happiness for this winter, we had the yellow fever a close neighbor this fall, quite a number of persons are a with at the Bend. Daughter & Doc got home safe but much frightened with the reports. I supposed you have heard before this of little William Henderson Peck, a most interesting personage I can assure you, nearly as pretty as your pet [*Ada*], she tells very often of you and the family, she remembers you all, she is as smart and as pretty as can be. We had the pleasure of hearing from you through Mr. Green' letter. Is Mr [Page 2] Washington entered into the "holy bonds of matrimony" yet. [?] that was the all absorbing topic when I left. and how does your Mother do [?]_ Well I hope. tell her we have had some weather for the last week that was cool enough for her; It has ben intensely cold, we have had summer weather all this fall, we have had a fine season for gathering cotton and make a fine crop, I know what a optimistic turn you have, and your kind heart makes you feel happy to hear of your friends doing well. But I do not believe that either you or Miss Cynthia would ever write a line, but one want to hear ever so much from you; I feel a great interest about that region of Wolf Creek where you live, and I think you might have dispensed with ceremony, do write soon and tell me how you are spending your time, I expect you are married. Daughter is making preparations for the summer's house [*Glen Ada*] keeping in making up bed and table linens, the Doctor is going to New Orleans in a few days to make purchases for Glen Ada house, Does it begin to look like a house to live in[?]. Tell your Mother she must not have the slightest touch of the hgtto? [Page 3] but must tidy? up her cheerfulness to attend the house warming when they get up.

None of us have been to the city this winter but Mr. Henderson, he is as fat and jolly as ever, our healthy climate agrees so well with him and Daughter I am afraid they will grow too fat. Little Willy is the best baby you ever saw. Daughter is so much taken up with her Babies, I now have no one to [help] work in the yard with me. I wish you could have seen the finest roses that were blooming ten days ago. Do you and Mr Green think of coming down, I can't see what prevents you, I wish you would. If Mr Washington is married present my best wishes and congratulations to him and his bride. Please give my love to your Mother and Miss Cynthia, my regrets to Mr Green, tell Miss Martha not to forget me for I may have to tax her strength and her patience again in climbing over the rocks with me. Mr. H would I know send his love to you all and perhaps with some saucy message if he was not fast asleep. So write soon, I would so much like to hear from you. Yours affectionately

Louise Henderson

[Page 4] [PS] Daughter and I seemed moved by the same spirit last night, I left a place in my letter for her to fill out to you, was the reason why I did not say more for her, not knowing that she was writing too. I hope you will write soon, but I will not wait for you, if ever I have anything to write, which I think will amuse you or serve to while away a tedious hour and [?] that [*night*]. I think very often of you all. May you live a thousand years and your shadow never grow less

November 14th [1857]

Dear Emma

Though I have been a sluggard In writing, it is no true reason that I have not thought often of you, I hope your Mother and the family are all well. Our little darlings were sick for some time after they got home, and some how they got somewhat spoilt, but Ada has a freicst? [phrase], which I think she must have learnt from your dear your Mother_ "Spare the whale bone and spoil the child". Mr Henderson had a little sick spell on his return home, he is so unused to sickness, that I can assure you, he was not patience personified.

I should like very much to hear from you, and I hope you will recollect, a line of remembrance is more acceptable than silence. We had a safe and pleasant trip home, no accident, no detention anywhere, and we travelled quite at our leisure. I heard from my sister [*Minerva*] to day, she was well, Lelia is going to school to a New York Lady, who is governess in their neighborhood, I suppose you have heard from Minerva before this, as she has to have written some time since, we have have [*sic*] had winter weather and summer weather, last week it was warm enough for muslin, which I wore; now it is cold enough for mirino. Rather for our cotton crops make, every one complains of [Page 2] of the shortness, but all hope to get fine prices not withstanding the "panic". Mr Henderson is now in the city, or rather on his way home, and I ought to have waited his return, to give you the news for the benefit of Mr Wash and Mr Green. We hope Mr Green will adhere to his promise, and come to see us this winter. Some of you ought to come. It is a pretty story that we all go to your house every day during the summer and receive all manner of kindness, and not one of you will return a visit. Has Cynthia accepted the Gent from the distant county, or has she thought it was a pity to make an interruption in that nice little family party that you have at home.[?]

Em I am afraid you thought of marrying when you sewed up all that stiff calico into quilts. Can you ever quilt them, you would make an excellent Catholic to inherit punishments on yourself for sins committed.

It was by the nearest chance Daughter and I miss a writing again to you on the same day, I have waited long enough to allow her letter to be read and to let this come in as something a little new, I wish I had some news to put in it to give you something to chat on around your cheerful evening fire. I often fancy to myself the silence that now surrounds Glen Ada; the evergreens must look beautiful but oh; the silence, it must be painful. [Page 3]

18th _ _ Since I commenced this a little stranger has made his appearance here by the name of Charles Talbot Peck. He was born on the 16th. Daughter thinks he is a great boy. and Willy is mighty put out because "Tarl" (for Charles) is not allowed to go to the table to eat of his favorite dish "Banes" (beans). Ada and Willy, without doubt are two brag children. I often tell Willy he will be as fat as your Ma, and he will laugh and say She eats so many berries. I hope she is well and as lively as ever, give my love to her and tell her to take good care of herself, and to Cynthia and tell her I would like very much if she would write me a good sociable letter, I know she has plenty of amusing things to make me laugh about, she is too fond of the ludicrous to let anything escape her. Mr Henderson got back from the city the day I communicated this which caused me to leave off where I did. He says hard times does not keep the ladies from shopping [.] It was impossible to enter some of the fashionable stores for the crowd of ladies. he sends his best respects to your Mother and to all of you. he says tell Mr Green he will have no difficulty in finding our Landing, If he gets on a Memphis boat, or indeed on any other, but it is at the foot of Island 18? on the Louisiana side. Do write to me soon as I am anxious

to hear from you and believe me truly yours   Louise
Henderson

Richmond August 4th [After 27 Mar 1859]

My Dear Miss Em

It did not seem right that I should stop through Tennessee without having been at your house, but when I think I of the sad changes that a few months have make, I am afraid that I have not the fortitude to go there without Daughter, and I feel too, that I want to see every place where my sweet little one played, her play places are holy ground to me. I felt like my heart would break when I saw the things you sent from Glen Ada_ comparing the past with the present, the desolating present. When I suddenly awake I think it is a dreadful dream that my darling my still be with us, and her loss has made me so anxious for Daughter and the other two little ones. I want to see you so we can talk about her, for I know you loved her. [Page 2]

Daughter having a new home, make us wander away off here, we went no further East than Washington City [*Tenn.*]. Minerva and Lilia is with us, and in the loss of my Dear Horace I have another source of deep misery, too hard to be realized. What a loss he is, his mother at times is very defected, and I am afraid, she thinks at times that I have no feeling_ when my heart aches almost to breaking, but I feel that I must not encourage a grief, I know will never end with her. If Mr H[enderson] will stop long enough, I will go with her to your house, but it will be a trial to both, for we cannot help recalling the time when we had those two dear ones with us_ the light and joy of our lives. We will leave here for the White Sulphur Springs [*West Virginia*]. Where we will stay as long as Mr H pleases, which I presume will not be long as he is anxious to return home, and I will go with him, but come again to see Daughter. In october, Minerva is afraid to go home so soon, and will remain either at your house or in Greenville [*TN or LA*]. I shall stop as I go on, to see Daughter. you ought [Page 3] to go down to see her oftener. I don't think Oakland half as pleasant as Dear Glen Ada. I was very glad to hear that your Mother was enjoying good health, how much I should like to see her, in truth I should like to see you all. give my love to her, and if I do not go now to see her I shall go when I come up in october. I do not know how I am to stay at home without Daughter, it makes me feel like the world has come to an end when I think of it. This is a pleasant place, and a beautiful place, and if it was nearer to Oakland I would get me a residence here, as I can't bear to live in the country without Daughter and the children.

Minerva and Mr H sends their kindest regards to your mother_ yourself and to Mr Wash and Mr Green. I would liked so much to have paid Cynthia a visit, but feeling that was improbile (sic), I never said anything about it. I hope Martha feels well and has grown to be more of a romp?.

With me_ you belong to the noncommitted club and never put pen to paper, never the less accept my [Page 4]

Sincerest regards

Yours affectionately
Louisa Henderson

November 19th 1860

My Dear Miss Em

I have been for a long time wishing to get a letter from you and to hear from you all. but I believe you will not write. and I am afraid you have not been to see my Daughter either. I hope your Mother keeps well, and is as lively as ever, tell her she must not mope this winter, and I will _ If I can _ prevent her doing so next summer. Mr H[enderson] says It will be too lonely to keep house at the glen next summer, but I would rather go there than any where else. My shrubbery is growing, I left a good part of it with Daughter. Minerva got home safe, she is very much pleased with her new servant. they have now some sickness among their negros. Mr Brown' carryall came into Vicksburg with the top covered over with coops filled with turkeys._ Just imagine how it looked. I expect Brown thinks his wife Is the greatest woman after getting him and "them" turkeys home safe.

I miss Daughter and the dear little ones much, sometimes I hardly know what to do with myself; and if a week passes without my getting a letter, I make sure some of them are sick. I will make a request of your Ma _ to make you write to me and let me know how she _ and you _ and all_ are. I can never forget how very kind you all have been, it seems you don't know how many obligations you can put one under. Mr. Wash' and Mr. Green' visit here I am afraid is all talk. Mr H sends his best respects to them and says he would be delighted to see them, please present my best respects to them, and tell them I have not seen a young lady this season that I think is good enough for either of them. I am going out soon to call a new young lady, and I will take a good look at her.

Em I wish you would make out a list of anything particular that you wanted from New Orleans, I would take great pleasure in filling it. When I go down, I will remember everything I see to tell you. So write soon if you please, I wish so much to hear from you. give my love to your Mother and I do hope she will keep well. and give my love to Mattie, and to Cynthia when you see her.

Most affectionately yours

Louise Henderson

Direct your letter to Omega_ Madison Parish _La we have a new post office.

January 26th 1861

My Dear Miss Em

I was really glad to get your letter, and to hear that you were all well. What a fine description you gave of the snow clad mountains, but it must have been very cold then, I can scarcely realize yours and Daughter's account of the deep snow, and it has been so warm here, but there has been a great deal of cloudy and rainy weather. I am afraid there will be high water in the spring, the [Mississippi] river now is very low, but I think all the levees in this Parish are good.

Well_ have not the fanatics of the North placed this country in a deplorable state, and not an united States soldier in it. In M[ississippi]. Guns have been placed on the bank at Vicksburg and no boat is allowed to pass, without first rounding to and showing her papers, it is to prevent boats bringing United States troops down. Cotton has to be brought from Mobile to Orleans for foreign shipment, as no ships can be cleared there now. I hope we will be able to sell and get off the rest of our cotton before New Orleans ports are closed. We had some mean cotton sold last week at 9 ½ ? cents. "They say" the ladies of New Orleans talk of [Page 2] shouldering their muskets and fighting in the ranks. and when I read the abuse, and see the fiendish wish those northern wretches have for ruining us, I feel as if I could fight every one I see pass here, they stop in very often to beg for something to eat_ but it may be to talk to the negros, as it is_ they go out faster than they come in. Mr H[enderson] shakes his head, and says he fears we are all to see trouble enough. people must have some confidence, as negros have sold pretty well in New Orleans. I met yesterday some of the newly elected members of the convention, waiting for a boat to take them to Baton Rouge, they are all hot Secessionists, and were in high spirits at the prospect of having nothing more to do with those vile wretches of the north. and I suppose in a few days Louisiana will be an Independent State, I gave them my heartiest wishes. out in Minvera's neighbourhood the War Spirit is most intense, she thought for a while it was a sinn?, but she and Mr R[hoton?] and Mr H[enderson] have all got over that weakness now. I was out to see her last month and she and Lelia were very well, she talked of taking Lelia to Nashville and placing her at Mr Elliot's school. She is still very much pleased with Caley? who has a baby. I did hope she would go with me and spend the summer at the Glen, but I cannot get either Mr H or her to consent to do that, he says he does not want to go the expense of moving servants. Mr H says we have made [Page 3] a good corn and cotton crop, we have not yet finished picking.

I am sorry you did not go to see Daughter, but I hope you will. Willy darling can now write me a letter himself. I am glad your Mother's health is good, and I hope it may long continue so, give her my best love and tell her to keep her cheerful temples in good repair to help her along. I am glad Cynthia has such a sweet little child to keep her company, be sure to always give my love to her. remember me to Mattie. I noticed you did not make a list of anything particular that you might want from New Orleans. I am afraid you will carry your independent feelings so far, that you would not say yes when you are asked to marry, you would think you would be concealing too much. Mr H sends his love to you all. he hates writing as bad [*as*] you or he would write to Mr Wash and Mr Green, but he says he will some of these days. Do write to me as it gives me pleasure to hear from you.

Most affectionately yours

Louise Henderson.

[PS] They told me yesterday there would be no difficulty in sending off cotton from Orleans, as there are foreign consuls living there. so we are all right. confusion to the Yankee fanatics, I almost hate anybody that speaks a word in favor of them. Daughter is a Disunionists too

Letter from Louise Henderson to Maggie Allen

Newport [TN]_ Mar 8th, [18]90

My Dear Maggie

       I have often thought of you and your Mother if I have not written. Mr. Holland dined with us while he was attending court, he said the children had all been sick with the grip? and now was threatened with whooping cough…and how sorry I was _ he said your Mother was not well. I did think it would be better if you all would conclude to spend a month or so some where, even a month at Mins' where you would be well entertained and would see every body, the change would do [Page 2] you good because you would see hear of people you know, better than to be off among strangers and there is always a something going on in this town. I suppose you know Miss Mary Myers has bought this house and takes a few boarders, she has not room for many, she wants day boarders. Mrs Anderson moved in that little 3 room house called Peterson's offices for lawyers & doctors, it was a bitter pill for him to have to go. Miss Mary sends her best love to you & your Mother and said she wishes you all would come and stay with her, I wish you would, you would be pleased as far as the eating and good cheerful company goes, I do wish she had better rooms, but you know hospitable people's [Page 3] houses have elastic walls, you must have a change.

How I have missed daughter, still I do not wish for her to return now as she is enjoying herself so well and dear Lee is there now [*in Sanford, FL*]. It almost made me sick to see him go, it made me feel so lonely. Dr Ed has been to see me since and sends me papers_ I was surprised Daughter keeps up her letters to Mrs Heiss who has been sick, but I suppose you still write to her_ may god bless and comfort her in spite of herself_ a Mrs Hall was buried yesterday she was a miss Vreams?. She left a young baby. Old Mr Deering died and was buried in the other snow storm. If Mrs Deering was to leave that house Miss Maria would be in a bad [Page 4] fix, she took me to be a fool, because I had been kind to her I suppose, told me "Mrs Fagula has paid all my bills" I would be safe to swallow in a lump? any she ever paid. I have been kind to "Vivian" and I did not take her abuse very well although I made her no reply, for I knew she would miss my solid services and when she came again would be in time_ I am ice to her now, but she sent yesterday for some late papers, I sent The Free Press: It got to be so trifling I spent? Sending it to you. Mr and Mrs Moss are boarding as day boarders with Miss Mary.

Give my love to your Mother, and she must think on what I proposed, she needs a change and so do you & the little darlings, give my love to your Mother and papers? to them. To think Mr "War?" will plan some way for you all to take a trip_ my kind regards to him. write soon of excuse my awful bad pen. Yours lovingly

L Henderson

Letter from Louise H. to Horace Prentice, Jr.[16]

November 20th [1857][17]

My Dear [*Nephew*] Horace

To say that I am uneasy would not begin to express how anxious I am at your long silence. The last letter I got from you said you had been sick, but I hope most earnestly that you are well now, and that you have a letter on the way to tell me so. I have tried to read my last letters to you, from memory to see if I have written anything to hurt you in "high audgeon?", but I can't, think I have, you know me too well. My dear good Horrey. I really feel so disappointed when they come from the office and say "no letter for you".

I have been very much employed, more so than usual, we have another little member of our house hold, who is not quite a week old, and is named Charles Talbot, he is a bright eyed little chap, Daughter [*Emma Peck*] sends her love to you, and she is very much pleased with the little Charley. I heard from your Mother [*Minerva*] not long since, Lelia had started to school on the ala grey house very happy: but I suppose you hear from her oftener than I do.

How do you come on, do write me a line to say that you are well and happy. I have no news to amuse you with, I hate to send a letter with nothing in it to you, but really I felt that [Page 2] I must write to let you know where I was living, so write soon. My eyes have failed me a good deal this week, but they feel better to night. Do you think of coming home, you must land here if you come. Next week I will try and scrape my wits? together and write you a longer and better letter. I hope that is if I can, my will is good to do so, but oh; my stupid head, and scratchy looking writing, my hand writing does look so falibian? It makes me nervous to look at it, therefore I never read my letters over.

I have had some good weather for cotton picking, but just at

---

[16] See Appendix 8 for Louise (Donohue) Henderson genealogy
[17] Year 1857 supplied based on details within the letter – Charles Talbot Peck was born 16 Nov 1857

this present time it is very cold. You are to night _ I hope _ sitting in a cozy comfortable, room, either with instructive books on with intelligent gentlemen, enjoying your hours quietly_ profitably and happily. and may you be always happy in the sincere wish of your affectionate aunt

Louise Henderson

I see by the papers uncle' place is to be sold the first of next month, I suppose Sanders will buy it. I have not heard one iota from Rebecca. I am so sorry she married so badly. I wish she would write to me

Letters from Emma E. Peck to Maggie Allen

Lake City [FL]
Nov 30th 1893

My Dear Maggie

At last! I send you the prescriptions for that good medicine for dysentery, I was telling you about. The dose is one teaspoonful every 3 or 4 hours, but it must be smaller doses for children. But I hope you will keep well, and won't need it. It seemed like I never was going to get it for you_ I had spoken to the Dr about it _ I saw him yesterday, and he told me that he wrote it for me, but when he looked in his pocket, he couldn't find it, so he wrote me another. The last letter I had from Miss Shier told me about Cynthia being sick _ I hope she soon got well, and will stay well all winter. This has been like a summer day. Ella [R. (King) Peck] had such a big Thanksgiving Turkey, and such a good dinner, and only one visitor to help us eat it. Tell the children I wish they could have seen what a show Richard [King Peck] made of himself this evening. He had a small shovel digging in the ash pile, and once, when he threw up a shovelful, it all came down on his head and face _ Oh! What a sight he was_ coal ashes too _ you could see his eyes looking so bright, and little patches of white face in different places _ but when he came out of his bath and dressed to go to the Depot, you would have hardly have thought it was the same child. For two or three days it was right cold here _ how was it with you? Mother [Louise Henderson] would say, "Oh! I know it is cold in Newport this morning" it would take such a little fire to warm us, and she would say if she was there, she would have to have such a big one. She sends her love to you and all, and says that now she is so far away from you, you all seem dearer than ever. [Page 3] We went visiting yesterday for the first time _ there have been so many things to prevent our going out _ after the diptheria was gone, we had cold weather and storms, that kept us in.   I sent to New York for some nice handkerechiefs for Louis and Lee, and when they come, I will take a trip to see them. Lee has been moved to Plant City [FL], and he likes it very well _ he is kept so busy, I have only had one letter from him.

     I forgot when I wrote last to tell about Mrs. Heiss' letter _ when I got to Newport I found it there, and I answered it from your house. Do you remember telling me to tell her that "you had been thinking of writing to her, to tell her, that she owed you a letter," but as I was writing, I could tell her.   A lady in town got up a "musical club" to help the College boys pay for their organ, by giving concerts_ they have given one, which was splendid_ some beautiful pieces were played, and I [Page 4] never heard Ella sing better. Mother said she was glad she went.   When I come, I will try to show you how one lady played _ or rather "pawed" and "clawed" _ it beat any sight I ever saw. The yard has been full of visitors today, to see the chickens_ it is a pretty sight_ about 600_ every one says they never saw such a sight in their lives.   It is Court week, and some one is here two or three times a day_ the incubators are great curiosities to them. Tell the children that the Parrot now sings_ "Pretty, pretty Polly Hopkins_ how do you do_oo_ how do you do" _ and she gets some kind of a tune to it. Ella says she would like to know, how in the name of goodness, she is going to wean Richard, when he comes and whispers to her _"Mamma tity"_ so pretty _ I think she would take it harder than he would, so I don't think he will be weaned for a year or two yet. Give my love to all, and write as soon as you can to

Your Loving Friend
Emma E. Peck

Lake City
Sept 6th 1894

My Dear Maggie

I was so glad to get your letter, and hope you are perfectly well now_ and also all the others. Tell Miss Cynthia I felt disappointed too, at not seeing you all, but I look forward to next summer. It doesn't look like Lee is ever going to be able to get off_ poor fellow has not had any help since June, and for about a week he was right sick, but never let me know it, until he was well_ he swung a hammock in his office, and would only get up to attend to the most important business. Capt King saw him the other day, and says he is looking every well. Paul has his hands so full, that I don't count on his being able to leave.

But I am going to count on Louis_ he is off for a month now_ he is a Knight of Pythias, and was in that grand Washington Parade_ then he went from there to Connecticut, where Fannie [(Perkins Gibbens) Peck – Wife of Louis] is.   Paul is selling milk and butter, and I think after while, will build up quite a trade. His cows are fixed so comfortably, and each one knows her stall. He is fixing up a beautiful home, and he has had so much work done out there _ he and Ella stay out there nearly all the time_ and Capt is gone, attending to railroad business, nearly all the time, so that leaves us_ Mrs. King, Gam and I to ourselves. Sometimes Capt says _ "Do you three old widows ever get lonesome? We tell him "no indeed". There has been a splendid Veterinary Surgeon here this summer, and I told him about your cows, and he gave me remedy, which I sent you_ but I hope you will have no more sick ones. When I told him about their throats swelling, he asked me "if their feet were sore" _ but I couldn't tell him. I received a short note from Miss Shier_ I see she and I can't agree about those "Heavenly Twins". Give my love to every one_ it was lively for Miss Cynthia this summer. Write when you can_ I know how full your hands are _ but I want to hear often from you.

Your Loving Friend
Emma E. Peck

[Prescription most likely included with 6 Sep 1894 Letter]

For Contagious Sore Throat

For Muriate of Snow? – one tablespoonful_
   Chlorate of Potash_ one tablespoonful _
Mix the two in a pint of water, and drench.
Repeat the dose every two hours.

If the mouth becomes sore, wash with
Hypersulphide of soda solution_
a tablespoonful to pint of water

Figure 48 - Western Union Telegram from Emma E. Peck to Maggie G. Allen regarding the death of Emma's mom, Louise Henderson,13 Feb 1897

13 Feb 1897

Received at L Rio,

Dated: Lake City, Fla.

To: Mrs. Maggie G. Allen

C/O Swan S. Burnett Del Rio Tenn.

Mother [*Louise Henderson*] died two forty five this afternoon.

                                  Emma E. Peck

Appendices

Appendix 1: Photo of the first page of *Ada's Journal*

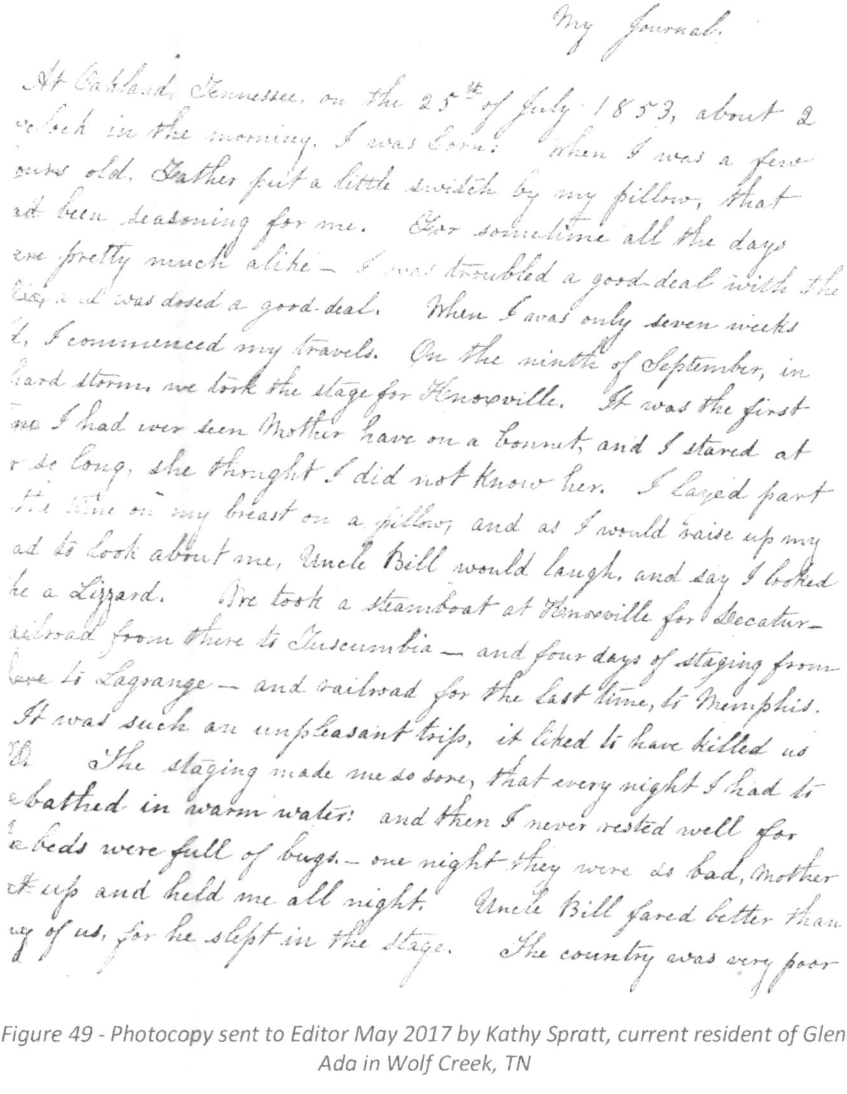

My Journal.

At Oakland, Tennessee, on the 25th of July 1853, about 2 o'clock in the morning, I was born. When I was a few hours old, Father put a little switch by my pillow, that he had been seasoning for me. For sometime all the days were pretty much alike — I was troubled a good deal with the colic, and was dosed a good deal. When I was only seven weeks old, I commenced my travels. On the ninth of September, in a hard storm, we took the stage for Knoxville. It was the first time I had ever seen Mother have on a bonnet, and I stared at her so long, she thought I did not know her. I layed part of the time on my breast on a pillow, and as I would raise up my head to look about me, Uncle Bill would laugh, and say I looked like a Lizzard. We took a steamboat at Knoxville for Decatur — railroad from there to Tuscumbia — and four days of staging from there to Lagrange — and railroad for the last time, to Memphis. It was such an unpleasant trip, it liked to have killed us all. The staging made me so sore, that every night I had to be bathed in warm water: and then I never rested well for the beds were full of bugs. — one night they were so bad, Mother got up and held me all night. Uncle Bill fared better than any of us, for he slept in the stage. The country was very poor

Figure 49 - Photocopy sent to Editor May 2017 by Kathy Spratt, current resident of Glen Ada in Wolf Creek, TN

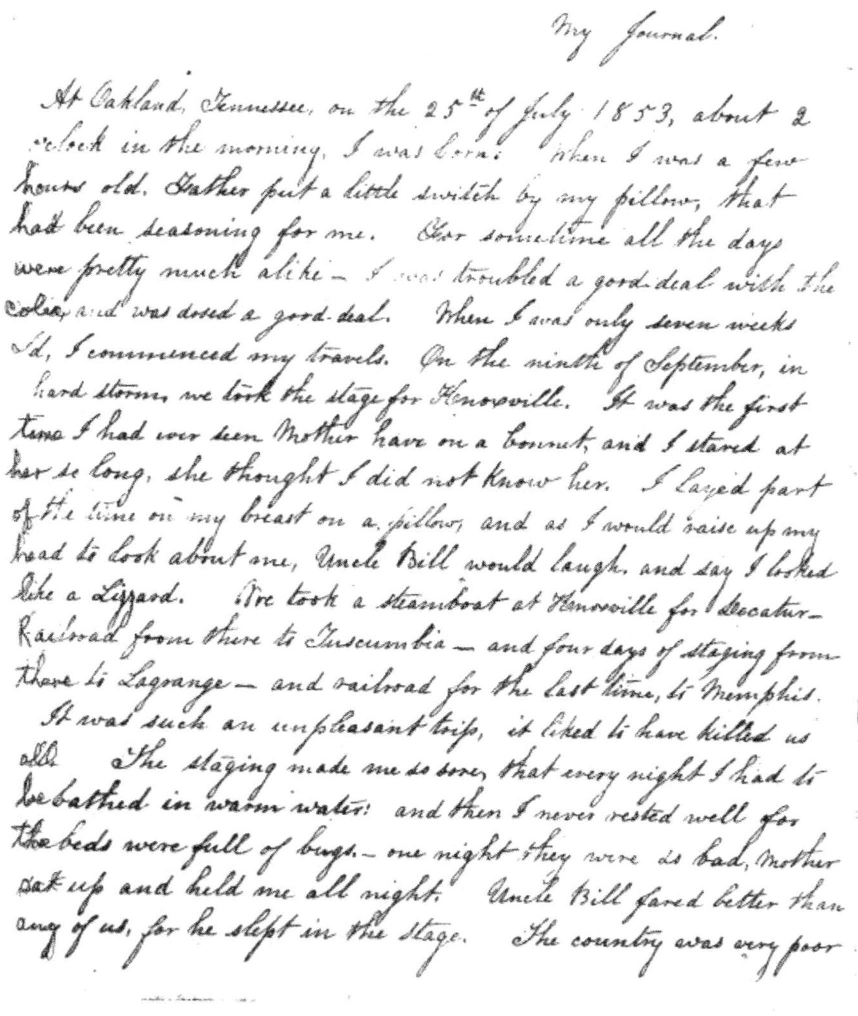

My Journal.

At Oakland, Tennessee, on the 25th of July 1853, about 2 o'clock in the morning, I was born. When I was a few hours old, Father put a little switch by my pillow, that had been seasoning for me. For sometime all the days were pretty much alike — I was troubled a good deal with the colic, and was dosed a good deal. When I was only seven weeks old, I commenced my travels. On the ninth of September, in hard storm, we took the stage for Knoxville. It was the first time I had ever seen Mother have on a bonnet, and I stared at her so long, she thought I did not know her. I layed part of the time on my breast on a pillow, and as I would raise up my head to look about me, Uncle Bill would laugh, and say I looked like a Lizzard. We took a steamboat at Knoxville for Decatur — Railroad from there to Tuscumbia — and four days of staging from there to Lagrange — and railroad for the last time, to Memphis. It was such an unpleasant trip, it liked to have killed us all. The staging made me so sore, that every night I had to be bathed in warm water: and then I never rested well for the beds were full of bugs. — one night they were so bad, Mother sat up and held me all night. Uncle Bill fared better than any of us, for he slept in the stage. The country was very poor.

Figure 50 - Jan 2021 Fresh Scan of Ada's Journal by Kyle Hovious of the Special Collections Dept at University of Tennessee-Knoxville. The editor is very thankful to Kyle for taking the time to make this scan. It helped reveal previously hidden words and phrases

Appendix 2: *Glen Ada* Poem by Mary Vance Clarke

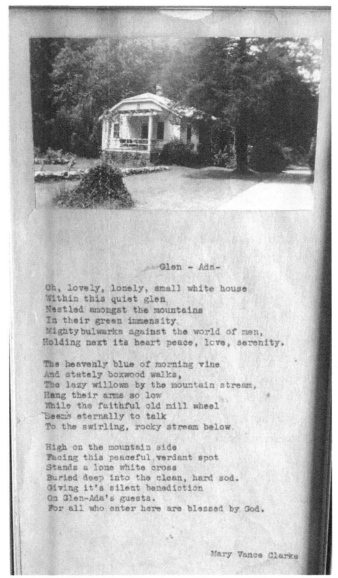

Glen - Ada-

Oh, lovely, lonely, small white house
Within this quiet glen
Nestled amongst the mountains
In their green immensity.
Mighty bulwarks against the world of men,
Holding next its heart peace, love, serenity.

The heavenly blue of morning vine
And stately boxwood walks,
The lazy willows by the mountain stream,
Hang their arms so low
While the faithful old mill wheel
Seems eternally to talk
To the swirling, rocky stream below.

High on the mountain side
Facing this peaceful, verdant spot
Stands a lone white cross
Buried deep into the clean, hard sod.
Giving it's silent benediction
On Glen-Ada's guests.
For all who enter here are blessed by God.

Mary Vance Clarke

Figure 51 - This poem, with a photo of the current Glen Ada home, hangs in Glen Ada. Photo of original by the editor 11 Jul 2017.

Glen – Ada –

Oh, lovely, lonely, small white house
Within this quiet glen
Nestled amongst the mountains
In their green immensity
Mighty bulwarks against the world of men,
Holding next its heart peace, love, serenity.

The heavenly blue of morning vine
And stately boxwood walks,
The lazy willows by the mountain stream,
Hang their arms so low
While the faithful old mill wheel
Seems eternally to talk
To the swirling, rocky stream below

High on the mountain side
Facing this peaceful, verdant spot
Stands a lone white cross
Buried deep into the clean, hard sod.
Giving it's silent benediction
On Glen-Ada's guests.
For all who enter here are blessed by God.

Mary Vance Clarke

Figure 52 - Photo of original Peck home in Wolf Creek, courtesy of Dede Rehkopf, ancestor of Ada's brother Paul Eve Peck, circa 1900

Appendix 3: Letter from Emma regarding Ada's death

Oakland April 22ᵈ 1859

My dear Miss Emma

I ought to have written long ago, but I could not. Have you heard that my dear darling Ada is dead — she was sick only a few hours, and died on the 27ᵗʰ March, at 8 oclock in the morning — O it was so hard to give her up — she had grown to be the best dearest little darling that ever was — She never seemed so well and bright as she did, the morning of the day she was taken sick, and about the middle of the day was suddenly taken with Cholera Morbus, we gave her some simple remedies, and thought she was better, but a fever came on at dark which lasted till next morning, when she died, so peacefully and without a pain — we could not get a doctor there till it was too late, and he said he could not have done her any good, that she had Congestion of the Brain, and he tells us now, that he has been watching Darling for a

Oakland April 22nd 1859

My dear Miss Emma

        I ought to have written long ago, but I could not. Have you heard that my dear darling Ada is dead _ she was sick only a few hours, and died on the 27th of March, at 8 o'clock in the morning _ O it was so hard to give her up _ she had grown to be the best dearest little darling that ever was _ She never seemed so well and bright as she did; the morning of the day she was taken sick, and about the middle of the day was suddenly taken with Cholera Morbus, we gave her some simple remedies, and thought she was better, but a fever came on at dark which lasted till next morning, when she died, so peacefully and without a pain _ we could not get a doctor there till it was too late, and he said he could not have done her any good, that she had Conjestion of the Brain, and he tell us now, that he has been watching darling for a [Page 2] long time, and knew we could not keep her with us. After she was dressed we kept her three days, she looked perfectly beautiful, I put fresh flowers round her every morning _ we have here a perfect likeness of her, that we had painted_ it looks like she was sleeping. She is in a beautiful metallic case, with a glass top, so we can look at her again, she is here with us, a vault is built in the yard here above ground, to put her in _ you don't know how broke up and lost we feel. After losing her down in that dreadful country, we got uneasy about our other children, and left home sooner than we expected _ I am not going back with them any more. I would like so much to see you, can't you come here, we are not going up to Glen Ada this summer, but I want to go and stay awhile at your house, some time this summer, Father here, told me when I wrote to you that I must beg you to come, and to be sure and make Mrs. Allen come with you, I wish you would, I want to see you both so much, I have so much to talk about my darling. Give my love to Mrs. Allen[,] Miss Martha & Miss Cynthia. Your affectionate friend   Emma E. Peck

long time, and knew we could not keep her with
us. After she was dressed we kept her three days,
she looked perfectly beautiful, I put fresh flowers round
her every morning — we have here a perfect likeness, of her,
that we had painted — it looks like she was sleeping.
She is in a beautiful Metallic case, with a glass top,
so we can look at her again, she is here with us, a
vault is built in the yard here, above ground, to put
her in — You don't know how broke up and lost we feel.
After losing her down in that dreadful country, we got
uneasy about our other children, and left home sooner
than we expected — I am not going back with them
any more. I would like so much to see you, can't
you come here, we are not going up to Glen Ida
this summer, but I want to go and stay awhile at
your house, some time this summer, Father here, told
me when I wrote to you, that I must beg you to come,
and to be sure and make Mrs Allen come with you,
I wish you would, I want to see you both so much, I have
so much to talk about my Darling. Give my love to Mrs Allen
Miss Martha & Miss Cynthia, Your affectionate friend
                                        Emma C. Peck

Appendix 4: Burning of the Bulletin No. 2

"The steamboat Bulletin No. 2, Capt. C. B. Church, was burned on the Mississippi river, near Islands No. 96 and 97, March 24th, 1855. A large quantity of cotton was among the freight, and this highly combustible article caused the flames to spread rapidly. The boat was run ashore as quickly as possible; but as soon as she struck the bank, she bounded back again, and floated down the river until consumed to the level of the water. The surface of the river was covered with floating bales of ignited cotton; and many persons who had leaped overboard, while attempting to save themselves by clinging to these fiery masses, were severely burned. One of the cabin passengers stated that he was sitting on the hurricane deck when the fire first appeared, and before he could get a bucket of water to throw on it, the whole boat seemed to be in a blaze. If the force pumps had been in good order, (which was not the case,) the flames could easily have been suppressed. An eye-witness thinks that the boat and the lives of many passengers could have been saved, if gum elastic hose had been provided for such an emergency. Certainly it shows shameful and criminal neglect on the part of the Captain or owners, when a steamer is without such apparatus. While the boat was burning, the passengers were greatly excited and dismayed; but we have one instance of surprising coolness, whether it proceeded from courage or stupidity, we will not pretend to say. A gentleman was standing in the cabin with perfect composure and apparent unconcern while the fire was making rapid progress in every direction. Capt. Church advised this stoical person to take off the door of a state room and endeavor to save himself thereon. "Make yourself easy, Captain,"

was the calm response, "I am safe enough !" And, sure enough, he was saved. This anecdote reminds us of one which is told of a celebrated gambler, who leaped from a burning boat into the Mississippi, exclaiming, "Now, gallows, save your own !"

Some of the passengers of the Bulletin succeeded in leaping on shore from the forecastle at the moment the steamer struck the land; but a large majority, who were in the after-part of the boat, were cut off from this means of escape. Capt. Church and all the other officers of the boat faithfully used every effort to save the passengers, and the Captain remained so long on board for this purpose, that his own life nearly became the sacrifice of his fidelity. When driven by the flames from the last refuge on the wreck, he threw himself in the water. The boat had drifted out to such a distance from the shore, that he would infallibly have been drowned, had not a skiff, which happened to be near, come to his assistance.

LIST OF THOSE WHO PERISHED.-Mr. Swick, Boston; C. Denny, deck hand; J. B. Williamson, New York; Jesper Brown, Friar's Point, Miss.; Orville Hill, Nashville; B. Handwerkt, Memphis, Tenn. John McConican, North Carolina; Evans Gwynn, Columbus, Ohio; a negro girl belonging to J. M. Craig, Arkansas; Nathaniel Carter, barber; Stephen Tareter, cabin-boy; four negro firemen, belonging to Capt. Church; several do. belonging to W. L. Porter, New Orleans; one negro fireman belonging to Mrs. Reinhart, Memphis, Tenn.; one do. belonging to J. R. Upsham, of same place, and an assistant engineer."[18]

---

[18] *Lloyd's Steamboat Directory: and Disasters On The Western Waters*, by James T. Lloyd, p 310-311, 1856, No copyright, special thanks to Univ. of Pittsburgh for making it available online:
https://digital.library.pitt.edu/islandora/object/pitt%3A31735054854082, accessed 4 Jan 2021

Appendix 5: Cholera Epidemic (1846-1860)

Editor's notes:
From Wikipedia[19]

"The **third cholera pandemic** (1846–60) was the third major outbreak of cholera originating in India in the nineteenth century that reached far beyond its borders, which researchers at UCLA believe may have started as early as 1837 and lasted until 1863. In Russia, more than one million people died of cholera. In 1853–54, the epidemic in London claimed over 10,000 lives, and there were 23,000 deaths for all of Great Britain. This pandemic was considered to have the highest fatalities of the 19th-century epidemics.

It had high fatalities among populations in Asia, Europe, Africa and North America. In 1854, which was considered the worst year, 23,000 people died in Great Britain.

That year, the British physician John Snow, who was working in a poor area of London, identified contaminated water as the means of transmission of the disease. After the 1854 Broad Street cholera outbreak he had mapped the cases of cholera in the Soho area in London, and noted a cluster of cases near a water pump in one neighborhood. To test his theory, he convinced officials to remove the pump handle, and the number of cholera cases in the area immediately declined. His breakthrough helped eventually bring the epidemic under control. Snow was a founding member of the Epidemiological Society of London, formed in response to a cholera outbreak in 1849, and he is considered one of the fathers of epidemiology.

---

[19] https://en.wikipedia.org/wiki/1846%E2%80%931860_cholera_pandemic, accessed 27 Feb 2021

Figure 55 - "It's Cholera to Blame" by Pavel Fedotov, 1854, Source
https://commons.wikimedia.org/wiki/File:Fedotov_cholera.jpg, accessed 26 Apr 2020

1840s

Over 15,000 people died of cholera in Mecca in 1846. In Russia, between 1847 and 1851, more than one million people died in the country's epidemic.

A two-year outbreak began in England and Wales in 1848, and claimed 52,000 lives. In London, it was the worst outbreak in the city's history, claiming 14,137 lives, over twice as many as the 1832 outbreak. Cholera hit Ireland in 1849 and killed many of the Irish Famine survivors, already weakened by starvation and fever. In 1849, cholera claimed 5,308 lives in the major port city of Liverpool, England, an embarkation point for immigrants to North America, and 1,834 in Hull, England. In 1849, a second major outbreak occurred in Paris.

Cholera, believed spread from Irish immigrant ship(s) from England to the United States, spread throughout the Mississippi river system, killing over 4,500 in St. Louis and over 3,000 in New Orleans. Thousands died in New York, a major destination for Irish immigrants. The outbreak that struck Nashville in 1849–1850 took the life of former U.S. President James K. Polk. During the California Gold Rush, cholera was transmitted along the California, Mormon and Oregon Trails as 6,000 to 12,000 are believed to have died on their way to Utah and Oregon in the cholera years of 1849–1855. It is believed cholera claimed more than 150,000 victims in the United States during the two pandemics between 1832 and 1849, and also claimed 200,000 victims in Mexico.

1850s

The cholera epidemic in Russia that started in 1847 would last until 1851, killing over one million people. In 1851, a ship coming from Cuba carried the disease to Gran Canaria. It is considered that more than 6,000 people died in the island during summer, out of a population of 58,000.

In 1852, cholera spread east to Indonesia, and later was carried to China and Japan in 1854. The Philippines were infected in 1858 and Korea in 1859. In 1859, an outbreak in Bengal contributed to transmission of the disease by travelers and troops to Iran, Iraq, Arabia and Russia. Japan suffered at least seven major outbreaks of cholera between 1858 and 1902. Between 100,000 and 200,000 people died of cholera in Tokyo in an outbreak in 1858–60.

In 1854, an outbreak of cholera in Chicago took the lives of 5.5 percent of the population (about 3,500 people). Providence, Rhode

Island suffered an outbreak so widespread that for the next thirty years, 1854 was known there as "The Year of Cholera." In 1853–54, London's epidemic claimed 10,739 lives. In Spain, over 236,000 died of cholera in the epidemic of 1854–55. The disease reached South America in 1854 and 1855, with victims in Venezuela and Brazil. During the third pandemic, Tunisia, which had not been affected by the two previous pandemics, thought Europeans had brought the disease. They blamed their sanitation practices. Some United States scientists began to believe that cholera was somehow associated with African Americans, as the disease was prevalent in the South in areas of black populations. Current researchers note their populations were underserved in terms of sanitation infrastructure, and health care, and they lived near the waterways by which travelers and ships carried the disease."

Appendix 6: When Wiley Peck killed Charles Harris

Ada's Uncle / Isham's Brother / Wiley [Hawkins] Peck
killed Charles N. Harris in self-defense with a bowie knife

From *Vincent's Semi-annual United States Register*, Pages 55-56, Jan 1860[20]

DREADFUL AFFRAY IN NEW ORLEANS. — This day, the crowded rotunda of the St. Charles Hotel, New Orleans, was thrown into the most intense state of excitement by a rencounter which took place there about one o'clock, or shortly before that hour, between Mr. Charles N. Harris, of Carroll parish, and Col. W. H. Peck, of Madison parish, a member elect of the State Legislature. The result of the difficulty was the killing of Harris by Col. Peck, who inflicted upon his person seven wounds, — three shot-wounds and four stab-wounds, two of which were necessarily fatal, as will be seen by the result of the examination made, and which appears below.

In order to give the whole facts of the case, we would state that, about a year ago, a difficulty occurred between the parties, in the parish of Madison, State of Louisiana, which led to some correspondence between the gentlemen, the exact result of which we are ignorant of. However, it appears that Mr. Harris came down to New Orleans a short time ago, and Col. Peck arrived also on the steamer Vicksburg, on her last trip down. The day before the murder, Col. Peck and a friend, with whom he came down to the city, came out from the gentle men's ordinary, where they had been dining, and proceeded to make their way through rather a large crowd into the centre of the rotunda.

---

[20] Vincent's Semi-annual United States Register: A Work in which the Principal Events of Every Half-year Occurring in the United States are Recorded, Each Arranged Under the Day of Its Date. This Volume Contains the Events Transpiring Between the 1st of January and 1st of July, 1860. United States: F. Vincent, 1860. Pp 55-56

While going through the crowd, Mr. Harris — who was unknown to the friend of Col. Peck — turned round and asked if they intended to insult him by pushing against him. Col. Peck's friend, thinking, from Harris's appearance, that he was drunk, replied, politely, that no one intended to insult him. Harris, while asking the question, looked at Col. Peck, who at once recognized him. Harris, after the answer given by Col. Peck's friend, and looking directly at Peck, said, as he placed his hand in his pocket, to the latter, "D — n you, you did intend to insult me." Harris, the moment he had finished speaking, drew a pistol and fired at Peck, who was in the act of placing his hand in his side-pocket for his pistol.

After firing and missing his aim, Harris turned and ran through the crowd; and Peck, seeing, doubtless, that he must kill innocent persons if he fired, desisted from so doing.

A short while after this affray, Harris was arrested, at the request of Mr. Hildreth, for disturbing the peace of the St. Charles Hotel, by firing a pistol in the rotunda, and locked up in the First District Station-House, where he remained until the following morning. When he was arrested, he had in his room a revolver, a Derringer pistol, and a bowie-knife, which were also taken to the station-house. He was arraigned before Recorder Summers and fined twenty dollars, which, upon paying, his weapons were handed back to him. When about taking them away, his attorney advised him not to put them in his pocket, but to wrap them up in a piece of paper and carry them in his hand ; which he did. He intended leaving the city that evening, and was at the window of the clerk's office of the St. Charles paying his bill when the difficulty recommenced.

Col. Peck, it is said, thought that Harris had left the city the previous evening, but was standing in the rotunda of the hotel when the baggage-master of the hotel, who knew him, said to him, "Colonel, there is the man who shot at you yesterday," (pointing at Harris;) and, probably supposing that Peck was not acquainted with him, added, "Don't molest him; for I am not positive he is the man." The baggage-master then passed up the stairs on the right-hand side. Col. Peck, it appears, on having his attention directed toward Harris, walked over from the stairs toward him, who, as we before stated, was paying his bill at the window, and halted a few paces from him, with his hands resting upon his hips.

At this juncture, Harris turned his head somewhat and saw him; and the statements of what occurred during the next few moments are somewhat conflicting. The clerk, Mr. Mayne, who had just handed Harris a ten-dollar bill in change, says that Peck looked for about a quarter of a minute at Harris, then a few words passed which he did not hear, and both drew about the same moment and fired ; but he thinks Col. Peck shot first. Others state that, as Col. Peck advanced toward Harris, the latter asked him if he intended taking advantage of him; that Peck replied, " You took advantage of me yesterday : I am armed, and I suppose you are;" that both then drew; some say that Peck shot a little in advance, some say that Harris shot first, and others that the reports were simultaneous. Another version of the affair is that Peck asked Harris if he was armed, and he, avoiding the question, replied, " I am not prepared to have a difficulty with you here, and I wish you would leave me;" and that both drew at once. However, the testimony which will be taken before the coroner will doubtless clear up this portion of the difficulty.

The firing having commenced, Harris retreated, and finally dodged into the door of the small bar and cigar room, and, shielding himself partly behind the glass door, looked out and tired from time to time. Two of his balls can be seen where they entered, — one in a pillar in a line with Peck, and another on the opposite side of the wall, — both high up. Peck, while Harris retreated, stepped out from the office, nearer to the dining-room, and fired several shots, — three of which took effect upon the person of Harris, — and was in that position when he was fired at from the room.

Exhausting his pistol, Peck drew his bowie-knife and deliberately advanced toward the door of the cigar-shop from behind which Harris had shot, and seemed to hesitate a moment whether to enter. The next moment, Harris, doubtless seeing his shadow upon the glass, fired at the open doorway, the ball of his pistol entering the side or jamb of the door.

After firing this last shot, Harris ran back just as Peck entered the door, got over the marble counter of the bar, and got into a corner among the bottles. Peck, following, sprang over after him, and, grasping hold of him, inflicted upon his person four stabs with the bowie-knife.

Thus ended this terrible rencounter. Harris was picked up and placed on the floor for a moment, and then carried to his room nearby, expiring almost the moment he was placed upon the bed. This account of the affair has been gathered through various persons who were present, though, from the great excitement which prevailed, there may have been things which were overlooked. The excitement was very intense, and most of the crowd got out of the way at the first firing. Some got behind pillars, others ran into the passages leading to the dining-room and ladies' parlor, and not a few, thinking it too late to fly, made shields of the chairs. A group of gentle men were standing conversing immediately in a line with the shot from Harris, which lodged in the wall a few feet above their heads. The accused was arrested, a short time after the killing, by Lieutenant Dryden, of the First District Police-Station. Col. Peck is a large, powerful-looking man, about six feet in height. The deceased was a man of ordinary stature and rather slight build.

The *post-mortem* examination was held by Dr. Bethelet, which showed the following wounds: — One shot-wound in the right shoulder ; two stab-wounds in the left arm ; one stab-wound in the left side, between the fifth and sixth ribs, penetrating the lungs : one shot-wound in the right side, between the seventh and eighth ribs, penetrating the liver; (these two wounds last above mentioned were the immediate cause of death ;) one shot-wound in the breast, between the first and second ribs.

Appendix 7: Obituary for Ada's Grandma Louise

Louise Donohue Henderson (Died 13 Feb 1897)

Died.

Mrs. Louise Henderson died at the residence of Mrs. J. D. Taylor on Saturday afternoon last. She had been sick for some time, and lay critically ill for several days before death claimed its own.

Mrs. Henderson, who was the mother of Mrs. Emma Peck, of this city, was born in St. Genevieve, Missouri, on March 4th, 1813, and was 84 years of age.

Her last illness was ministered to by many kind friends of Lake City, as well as her grandchildren, Messrs. R. L. Peck and Louis S. Peck, and wife.

Among her relatives and friends Mrs. Henderson was affectionately known as "Gam," and her cheerful and considerate manner gained for her friends, in all her household, who regarded her as an "optimist." Her ready humor and bright intellect, which, constantly, drew on a large store house of knowledge, made her always a most agreeable companion.

Rev. D. W. Humphreys officiated at the funeral, which was largely attended, despite the very disagreeable weather.

The sympathy of the community goes out to the bereaved family.

Figure 56 - Obituary for Louise Henderson, Unknown newspaper, Date circa 13 Feb 1897, Clipping from Betty Walker Collection, Used with Permission

Died.

Mrs. Louise Henderson died at the residence of Mrs. J. D. Taylor on Saturday afternoon last. She had been sick from some time, and lay critically ill for several days before death claimed its own.

Mrs. Henderson, who was the mother of Mrs. Emma Peck, of this city, was born in St. Genevieve, Missouri, on March 4th, 1813, and was 84 years of age.

Her last illness was ministered to by many kind friends of Lake City, as well as her grandchildren, Messrs. R.[obert] L.[ee] Peck and Louis S.[harkey] Peck, and wife [*"Fannie" Perkins (Gibbens) Peck*].

Among her relatives and friends Mrs. Henderson was affectionately known as "Gam," and her cheerful and considerate manner gained for her friends, in all her household, who regarded her as an "optimist." Her ready humor and bright intellect, which, constantly, drew on a large store house of knowledge, made her always a most agreeable companion.

Rev. D. W. Humphreys officiated at the funeral, which was largely attended, despite the very disagreeable weather.

The sympathy of the community goes out to the bereaved family.

Appendix 8: Louise (Donohue) Henderson Genealogy[21]

Elizabeth Pettit (b. 15 Jun 1779 - d. 27 Nov 1827)

Figure 57 - Headstone for Elizabeth [Pettit] Donohue, buried in Hopewell Cemetery, Warrenton, MS, Photo by Janie Fortenberry, 27 Aug 2014, posted to https://www.findagrave.com/memorial/26728156/elizabeth-donahue/photo

ELIZABETH PETTIT was born in 15 Jun 1779 at Pettit's Station, Lincoln Co., Kentucky, and died 27 Nov 1827 in Vicksburg, Mississippi, buried in Hopewell Cemetery next to her parents. She

[21] http://freepages.rootsweb.com/~passages/genealogy/Elizabeth.html, accessed 25 Apr 2020

married **JOHN DONOHUE** 13 Nov 1802, in St. Genevieve, MO, son of **JOSEPH DONOHUE** and **NANCY VAUGHLEN**. He was born about 1770 in Pennsylvania, and died after 1829.

John Donohue [*Emma E. (Henderson) Peck's Uncle*] was named administrator of his wife's estate on June 21, 1828; Horace Prentice [*Emma Henderson's Uncle*] was bondsman for $100. A year later, the court made note that Donohue had not made an inventory. He moved away from Warren County before the 1830 census was taken.

Marriage notes: Sainte Genevieve Marriages, Baptisms, and Burials From the Church Registers, Some Marriages from the Court House Records, and a List of Inscriptions from the Protestant Burying Grounds, 1759-1839, made by Mrs. Ida M. Schaaf and by her Presented to the Missouri Historical Society, 1918. Jefferson Memorial St. Louis, MO 1918.

Page in Schaaf [*files*] (cut off of copy), pages 75-76 in Church Record: 1802 Nov. 13th **Donohue, John**, son of **Joseph Donohue** and **Nancy Vaughlen**, native of Pennsylvania, of the Presbyterian religion to **Pettit, Elizabeth**, daughter of **Benjamin Pettit** and **Rebecca Lorimor**, native of Kentucky of the Presbyterian religion. Witnesses: **Benjamin Pettit**, **Samuel Donnohue**; **Ezekiel Fenwick**; **C Anthony** with Maxwell

Children of **ELIZABETH PETTIT** and **JOHN DONAHUE** are:

       i.   **JOHN DONAHUE**, b. 1803. John married and lived on Bayou La Fourche in South Louisiana.

       ii.   **LOUISA DONAHUE**, b. 1805 [*conflicts with 1813 date given in obituary*]; m. **WILLIAM HENDERSON**, December 13, 1827, Warren, MS.

       iii.   **MILTON DONAHUE**, b. 1807. Cause of Death: Drowned while swimming in Mississippi River

iv. **MINERVA B. DONAHUE**, b. 1808. She married **HORACE PRENTICE** 8 Jan 1828, in Vicksburg, (Warren Cty.) MS, son of **JOSEPH PRENTICE** and **PRISCILLA MERRIMAN** of Grafton Ma. Brother of Maria Prentice of Grafton, MA (wife of William McDowell Pettit, early settler of KY, MO, MS and Lake Village AR). They are descendants of Henry Prentice, the planter of Cambridge, MA, Massachusetts Bay Colony (abt. 1640) and the early New England Settlers Merrimans of Concord, MA. and Pilgrim Deacon Edmund Rice of Sudbury, MA and Richard Sartell (Sawtell) of Groton, MA.

Listed on census: 1830, Ouachita Parish, LA with Walker Pettit, William McDowell Pettit, Francis Pettit, and James Newton Pettit.

Children of **MINERVA DONAHUE** and **HORACE PRENTICE** are:

a. **JOSEPH PRENTICE**, b. 6 Jun 1829, Warrenton, MS; d. September 15, 1855, Mississippi City, LA. Died during a hurricane and is buried in Hopewell Cemetery next to his grandmother, Elizabeth and great grandparents, Benjamin and Rebecca. Joseph is listed on the 1850 census for Warren City., MS

b. **LOUISA PRENTICE**, b. Jan. 1833, Lake Providian, LA; d. 3 Jun 1835, Lake Providian, LA. Published in the Vicksburg Register - June 1835 - Wm. Mills editor Died on 3d at Lake Providian, Parish of Carrol, LA, of the measles, Louisa Ann, daughter of Horace and Minerva Prentice - aged 2 yrs and 5 mos.

c. **REBECCA DONAHUE**, d. Convent school in Bardstown, KY.

Figure 58 - Tombstone for Joseph Prentice, Old Hopewell Cemetery, Warrenton, MS. Inscription reads: "To the memory of Joseph Prentice BORN in Warrenton, Miss. June 6, 1829 DIED in Mississippi City by the falling of a house Sept. 15, 1855." Photo by Janie, http://southernlagniappe.blogspot.com/2011/09/old-hopewell-cemetery-warren-county-ms.html, accessed 9 Apr 2021

❖ Additional genealogical descendant reports can be found in forthcoming titles by Cross Mountain Books in The Pecks of Mossy Creek series. Two planned books, *Sawbones* and *He Loved the Folks*, listed at the end of this volume.

❖ For a genealogy including Adam Peck, Sr. and his children, see the Addendum to *Adam the Younger, 1791-1866, And the War of 1812, The "Second Revolutionary War," The Peck Clan in America, Volume II, Part One* by Susan Moore Teller.

Appendix 9: General William Raine Peck

Ada's Uncle, William Raine Peck, was known as the largest Civil War general and often called "Big Peck." He was the final commander for the famed Louisiana Tigers. As evidenced by the journal, he loved his little niece Ada. He showered her with gifts including bales of cotton (to be sold for profit) and even a talking parrot named Polly. When he died in 1871, the Vicksburg Herald published a lengthy obituary. It can be found in *The Daily Telegraph* from Monroe, LA, published 27 Jan 1871 on page 2. It reads:

[From the Vicksburg Herald.
Death of General Wm. R. Peck.

Our entire community will learn, with unaffected regret, of the sudden and unexpected death of that gallant soldier and true hearted gentlemen, General William R. Peck. This sad event occurred at 8 o'clock yesterday morning, at the late residence of the General, in Madison parish, La., and was, we learn, produced by a congestive chill. General Peck was about forty-seven years of age, and was possessed of as many noble and generous qualities as usually fall to the lot of man. He was widely known, and where he was known the best, he was most highly esteemed and warmly beloved. He has hosts of friends to whom his qualities had endeared him, and his death will produce a pang in many hearts now widely scattered.

General Peck was born in East Tennessee, but his boyhood was spent in this city, with his elder brother, Dr. [Isham] Peck. When he arrived at manhood, he removed to the parish of Madison, La., where, with the energy peculiar to him, he engaged in planting. His success as a planter was signal and brilliant, and a few years saw him the master of a fortune, which his own judgment and industry had accumulated. A Democrat in politics, he took an active part in the political struggles of the day, and on several occasions was chosen by the people to represent Madison parish in the Legislature of Louisiana, where his excellent sense, sound judgement, genial manners and generous impulses, gave him a commanding influence. He had been warmly recommended for the office of Chief Magistrate of Louisiana, and but for the occurrence of the war, we doubt not that he would long since have been chosen the Governor of that great State.

When hostilities between the North and the South commenced, he saw plainly what duty required, and like the brave gentleman he was, he prepared to tread in its thorny path. He raised a company of volunteers, of which he was unanimously chosen Captain, and his company was assigned to Colonel (subsequently Lieutenant-General) Richard Taylor, as a portion of the 9th Regiment. How he discharged the duties of a soldier, we all know. He rose to the Colonelcy of his regiment, became a Brig.-General, and if the war had lasted three months longer, would have worn the rank of a Major General. Distinguished for personal gallantry in the army, that of Northern Virginia, where personal gallantry was the rule, his tall form and Herculean proportions made him concpicuous [*sic*] on every battle-field, and his plume, like that of Henry of Navarre, was always in the lead, and in the thickest of the fight. To his old comrades in arms, the intelligence of his death will come with the force of a personal bereavement, and there is not one who shared with him the dangers and the glories of the campaigns of Gen. Lee, who will not drop a tear to the memory of General William R. Peck, as brave a soldier, and as generous a gentleman, as ever wore a sword, or bestrode a horse. Peace to the memory of the gallant dead.

Figure 59 - General William Raine Peck, Photo by S. Anderson Photographer, New Orleans, LA, circa 1863, public domain.

Presidential Pardon

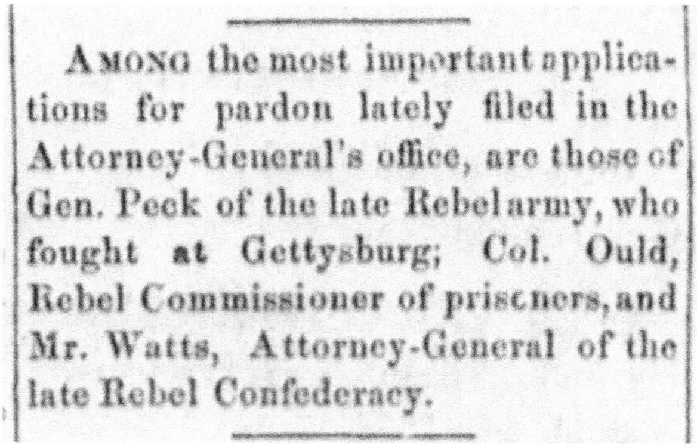

AMONG the most important applica-
tions for pardon lately filed in the
Attorney-General's office, are those of
Gen. Peck of the late Rebel army, who
fought at Gettysburg; Col. Ould,
Rebel Commissioner of prisoners, and
Mr. Watts, Attorney-General of the
late Rebel Confederacy.

Figure 60 - 12 Oct 1865 The Tiffin Tribune (Tiffin, OH) Pg 3

The Tiffin Tribune (Tiffin, OH) Pg 3, 12 Oct 1865

"AMONG the most important applications for pardon lately filed in the Attorney-General's office, are those of Gen. Peck of the late Rebel army, who fought at Gettysburg; Col. Ould, Rebel Commissioner of prisoners, and Mr. Watts, Attorney-General of the late Rebel Confederacy."

The Chicago Tribune (Chicago, IL) Pg 1, 12 Oct 1865

"To-day there was a larger crowd of visitors at the White House than at any time for a week past. The interview seekers were principally females. Mrs. Stephen A. Douglas and Mrs. Surgeon General Barnes were both granted special interviews with the President [Andrew Johnson]. But a limited number of pardon seekers attended, the only one of any note being ex-rebel Gen. Peck. [. . .]

The number of applications for pardon filed at the Attorney General's office up to date is about 27,000. About 7,000 pardon warrants have been signed by the President. The applications received average about 400 a day."

Index

Cross Mountain Books

In addition to *Ada's Journal and Emma's Letters*, enjoy these forthcoming titles from Cross Mountain Books in The Pecks of Mossy Creek series. Enter coupon code **ADASJOURNAL2021** at checkout for 10% off!

Sawbones: The Life and Times of Dr. Isham Talbot Peck

Between 1874 and 1886, Dr. Isham Peck (grandson of Adam Peck, Sr. founder of Mossy Creek) wrote letters to the editor of *The Morristown Gazette* under the pen name Sawbones, and people wrote to him as well. *Sawbones* takes you on a deep dive into life in East Tennessee and Northeastern Louisiana during the years of Reconstruction after the Civil War and beyond. *Sawbones* expresses his thoughts on politics, agriculture, church, friendship, and fishing. Author/Editor Andy Peck includes the history of Isham Peck and family, including what is known about his pre-Civil War service in the U.S. Army as a surgeon. Allow yourself to be transported to places like Wolf Creek, TN as the author includes a series of videos recorded at places where Isham and family lived. *Sawbones* is a journey worth experiencing!

ISBN 9781955121088 (pbk) | ISBN 9781955121095 (hardcover)

He Loved the Folks: Dr. Edward Jerome Peck of Hot Springs, NC by Andy Peck

In *He Loved the Folks*, learn how this doctor from Wolf Creek, TN gently influenced the entire area around Hot Springs, NC for good by his steady, faithful, medical service. Dr. Ed Peck (son of Dr. Isham T. Peck) was so loved at the time of his death, that the community came together and erected a monument to honor his life and love. He doctored such notable people as Jane (Hicks) Gentry, and served important Hot Springs institutions including the Dorland Institute, Mountain Park Hotel, and the Southern Railway Surgeons Association. In *He Loved the Folks*, you will catch a glimpse as to why this man was so loved by the Hot Springs community, as he dedicated his life to them.

ISBN 9781955121040 (pbk) | ISBN 9781955121057 (hardcover)

Cross Mountain Books™

www.crossmountainbooks.com

Made in the USA
Columbia, SC
29 June 2021

41141822R00095